Joint Meeting of SIGMORPHON and SIGFSM

(MORPHFSM 2014)

Held at ACL 2014

Baltimore, Maryland, USA
27 June 2014

ISBN: 978-1-63439-208-2

Printed from e-media with permission by:

Curran Associates, Inc.
57 Morehouse Lane
Red Hook, NY 12571

Some format issues inherent in the e-media version may also appear in this print version.

Printed by Curran Associates, Inc. (2014)

For permission requests, please contact the Association for Computational Linguistics at the address below.

Association for Computational Linguistics
209 N. Eighth Street
Stroudsburg, Pennsylvania 18360

Phone: 1-570-476-8006
Fax: 1-570-476-0860

acl@aclweb.org

Additional copies of this publication are available from:

Curran Associates, Inc.
57 Morehouse Lane
Red Hook, NY 12571 USA
Phone: 845-758-0400
Fax: 845-758-2634
Email: curran@proceedings.com
Web: www.proceedings.com

Preface

These proceedings contain the contributions presented at the MORPHFSM workshop held on June 27, 2014 in conjunction with ACL 2014 in Baltimore, Maryland, USA. The workshop was a joint meeting of two special interest groups of the ACL:

- SIGMORPHON — the special interest group in computational morphology, phonology and phonetics, and
- SIGFSM — the special interest group on finite-state methods.

It was the thirteenth meeting of SIGMORPHON and an off-year event for SIGFSM. The full-day workshop consisted of an invited presentation by JASON EISNER, contributed presentations, and a special panel session on open problems.

The workshop covered a wide range of topics from theoretical to applied morphology and finite-state technology in natural language processing. This volume contains the 7 regular and 1 panel paper that were presented at the workshop. In total, 12 papers (10 regular and 2 panel papers) were submitted to a doubly blind refereeing process, in which each paper was reviewed by 3 program committee members. The overall acceptance rate was 67%. The program committee was composed of internationally leading researchers and practitioners selected from academia, research labs, and companies.

The organizing committee would like to thank the program committee for their hard work and valuable feedback, the invited speaker JASON EISNER for his innovative and inspiring keynote, our panelists for their interesting discussion and expertise, the local organizers for their tireless efforts, the ACL administration for their support, and last but not least the authors for their contributions.

ÖZLEM ÇETINOĞLU
JEFFREY HEINZ
ANDREAS MALETTI
JASON RIGGLE

Organizers:

Özlem Çetinoğlu, IMS, University of Stuttgart (Germany)
Jeffrey Heinz, University of Delaware, Delaware (USA)
Andreas Maletti, IMS, University of Stuttgart (Germany)
Jason Riggle, University of Chicago, Illinois (USA)

Program Committee:

Adam Albright, MIT (USA)
Lynne Cahill, University of Sussex (UK)
Francisco Casacuberta, Instituto Tecnológico de Informática (Spain)
Jason Eisner, Johns Hopkins University (USA)
Roger Evans, University of Brighton (UK)
Sharon Goldwater, University of Edinburgh (UK)
Colin de la Higuera, University of Nantes (France)
Mans Hulden, University of Helsinki (Finland)
André Kempe, Nuance Communications (Germany)
Grzegorz Kondrak, University of Alberta (Canada)
Kimmo Koskenniemi, University of Helskinki (Finland)
Marco Kuhlmann, Linköping University (Sweden)
Karen Livescu, Toyota Technological Institute at U. Chicago (USA)
Giorgio Magri, IJN, ENS (France)
Mark-Jan Nederhof , University of St. Andrews (UK)
Kemal Oflazer, Carnegie Mellon University (Qatar)
Katya Pertsova, University of North Carolina (USA)
Max Silberztein, Université de Franche-Comté (France)
Richard Sproat, Google (USA)
Shuly Wintner, University of Haifa (Israel)
Anssi Yli-Jyrä, University of Helsinki (Finland)
Kristine Yu, University of Massachussetts, Amherst (USA)

Invited Speaker:

Jason Eisner, Johns Hopkins University (USA)

Panelists:

Jason Eisner, Johns Hopkins University (USA)
Mans Hulden, University of Helsinki (Finland)
Grzegorz Kondrak, University of Alberta (Canada)
Jason Riggle, University of Chicago, Illinois (USA)

Table of Contents

Conference Program

Keynote session

9:00–9:15 Welcome by Jason Riggle

9:15–10:15 Keynote by Jason Eisner

10:30–11:00 Morning break

Morning session

11:00–11:30 *Revisiting Word Neighborhoods for Speech Recognition*
Preethi Jyothi and Karen Livescu

11:30–12:00 *The Error-driven Ranking Model of the Acquisition of Phonotactics: How to Keep the Faithfulness Constraints at Bay*
Giorgio Magri

12:00–12:30 *Comparing Models of Phonotactics for Word Segmentation*
Natalie Schrimpf and Gaja Jarosz

12:30–14:00 Lunch break

Early afternoon session

14:00–14:30 *Generalizing Inflection Tables into Paradigms with Finite State Operations*
Mans Hulden

14:30–15:00 *Automatic Conversion of Dialectal Tamil Text to Standard Written Tamil Text using FSTs*
Marimuthu K and Sobha Lalitha Devi

15:00–15:30 *Rule Based Morphological Analyzer of Kazakh Language*
Gulshat Kessikbayeva and Ilyas Cicekli

15:30–16:00 Afternoon break

No Day Set (continued)

Afternoon session

16:00–16:30 *Rules, Analogy, and Social Factors Codetermine Past-tense Formation Patterns in English*
Peter Racz, Clayton Beckner, Jennifer B. Hay and Janet B. Pierrehumbert

Panel discussion

16:30–16:40 *10 Open Questions in Computational Morphonology*
Grzegorz Kondrak

16:40–17:30 Panel discussion by Jason Eisner, Mans Hulden, Grzegorz Kondrak, Jason Riggle

Revisiting Word Neighborhoods for Speech Recognition

Preethi Jyothi[*]
Beckman Institute
University of Illinois, Urbana, IL
pjyothi@illinois.edu

Karen Livescu
Toyota Technological Institute at Chicago
Chicago, IL
klivescu@ttic.edu

Abstract

Word neighborhoods have been suggested but not thoroughly explored as an explanatory variable for errors in automatic speech recognition (ASR). We revisit the definition of word neighborhoods, propose new measures using a fine-grained articulatory representation of word pronunciations, and consider new neighbor weighting functions. We analyze the significance of our measures as predictors of errors in an isolated-word ASR system and a continuous-word ASR system. We find that our measures are significantly better predictors of ASR errors than previously used neighborhood density measures.

1 Introduction

An important pursuit for both human and machine speech recognition research is to understand the factors that affect word recognition accuracy. In the substantial body of work on human word recognition, it has been shown that it is harder to recognize words that have many "similar" neighboring words than words with few neighbors (Luce and Pisoni, 1998), and that frequent words are recognized faster and more accurately than are infrequent words (Marslen-Wilson, 1987; Luce and Pisoni, 1998; Vitevitch and Luce, 1999). In the ASR research community, prior work has also investigated various factors that benefit or disrupt recognition. Examples of such factors include word frequency, speaking rate, and prosodic factors (Fosler-Lussier and Morgan, 1999; Shinozaki and Furui, 2001; Hirschberg et al., 2004; Goldwater et al., 2010). There has also been prior work that uses word confusability measures to predict speech recognition errors (Fosler-Lussier et al., 2005; Jyothi and Fosler-Lussier, 2009).

[*]Supported by a Beckman Postdoctoral Fellowship.

Word neighborhood measures have been studied more heavily for human word recognition than as predictors of ASR errors. Although not studied specifically in prior work (Fosler-Lussier et al., 2005; Jyothi and Fosler-Lussier, 2009), word confusability measures used in predicting ASR errors could be utilized to build word neighborhoods. Goldwater et al. (2010) examine the behavior of certain standard neighborhood density measures as predictors of ASR errors. To our knowledge, this is the only study that explicitly considers word neighborhoods as a potential factor in ASR.

In this work, we investigate word neighborhood measures as predictors of ASR errors. We propose new neighborhood measures that we find to be more well-suited to ASR than standard neighborhood density measures. We also propose a new mechanism to incorporate frequency weighting within the measures. Finally, we analyze the measures as predictors of errors in an isolated-word recognition system and a continuous-word recognition system for conversational speech.

2 Related Work: Neighborhood Density Measures

In much of the prior work in the psycholinguistics literature, the notion of word similarity is quantified by a simple one-phone-away rule: A word w' is a neighbor of word w if w and w' differ by a single phone, via a substitution, deletion, or insertion. We refer to this density measure as "**ND**".

$$\mathrm{ND} = \sum_{w'} \overline{\Delta}_{\mathrm{ND}}(w, w')$$

where $\overline{\Delta}_{\mathrm{ND}}(w, w') = 1$ if w and w' differ by a phone and 0 otherwise.

The frequencies of the neighbors are often accounted for in the neighborhood density measure by computing the sum of the raw (or log) frequencies of a word's neighbors (Luce and Pisoni, 1998; Vitevitch and Luce, 1999); the word frequencies

Proceedings of the 2014 Joint Meeting of SIGMORPHON and SIGFSM, pages 1–9,
Baltimore, Maryland USA, June 27 2014.

are derived from a large corpus. We refer to this frequency-weighted measure as "**wND**".

$$\text{wND} = \sum_{w'} \overline{\Delta}_{\text{ND}}(w, w') \cdot \pi(w')$$

where $\pi(w')$ is the frequency of the word w'.[1] Both **ND** and **wND** are popular measures for word neighborhoods that we consider to be our baselines; Goldwater et al. (2010) also make use of these two density measures.[2]

Neither of these measures account for the frequency of the word itself. In continuous ASR, which uses a language model, frequent words are more likely to be recognized correctly (Fosler-Lussier and Morgan, 1999). To account for this, instead of using absolute frequencies of the neighboring words, we use their relative frequencies to define a third baseline density measure,"**rwND**" (relative-**wND**):

$$\text{rwND} = \sum_{w'} \overline{\Delta}_{\text{ND}}(w, w') \cdot \frac{\pi(w')}{\pi(w)}$$

Relative frequencies have appeared in prior work (Luce, 1986; Luce and Pisoni, 1998; Scarborough, 2012). In fact, the measure used by Scarborough (2012) is the reciprocal of rwND.

3 Proposed Neighborhood Measures

Our new neighborhood measures are defined in terms of a distance function between a pair of words, Δ, and a weighting function, β. The proposed measures are not densities in the same sense as **ND, wND, rwND**, but are scores that we may expect to correlate with recognition errors. We define the neighborhood score for a word w as:

$$\text{score}(w) = \sum_{w' \neq w} \beta(w, w') \cdot \Delta(w, w') \qquad (1)$$

Intuitively, β is an averaging function that weighs the importance of each neighboring word. For example, Yarkoni et al. (2008) use a neighborhood measure that gives equal importance to the top 20 closest neighbors and rejects the others. The rest of the section presents multiple choices for Δ and β which will define our various neighborhood measures via Equation 1.

3.1 Distance Functions

All of our distance functions are based on an edit distance between a pair of words, i.e., the minimum cost incurred in converting one word to the other using substitutions, insertions and deletions of the sub-word units in the word. In addition to binary edit costs, we consider edit costs that depend on sub-phonetic properties of the phones rather than a uniform cost across all phones. Second, instead of a single pronunciation for a word, we consider a distribution over multiple pronunciations. These distance functions can be easily computed via finite-state transducer (FST) operations, as explained below (see also Figure 1).

Edit Distance (Δ_{ED}): This is the simplest edit distance function that incurs an equal cost of 1 for any substitution, insertion, or deletion. To compute the distance between a pair of words, each word w is represented as a finite state acceptor, F_w, that accepts the pronunciations (phone sequences) of the word. We also introduce a memoryless transducer, T, that maps an input phone to any output phone, with arc weights equal to the corresponding substitution costs (mapping to or from epsilon indicates a deletion or an insertion). The weight of the shortest path in the composed FST, $F_w \circ T \circ F_{w'}$, gives the edit distance between w and w'. When either w or w' has more than one pronunciation, Δ_{ED} is the minimum edit distance among all pairs of pronunciations. This edit distance function has been previously proposed as a measure of phonological similarity between words (Hahn and Bailey, 2005). Similar distance functions have also been used for neighborhood density measures in visual word recognition studies (Yarkoni et al., 2008).

Simple Articulatory Feature-based Edit Distance (Δ_{AF}): The distance function Δ_{ED} penalizes an incorrect substitution equally regardless of the phone identity; for example, the phone [p] can be substituted with [b] or [aa] with equal cost according to Δ_{ED}, although we know it is more likely for [p] to be produced as [b] than as [aa]. To account for this, we adopt a finer-grained representation of the phone as a vector of discrete articulatory "features". Our features are derived from

[1] Here we use raw rather than log frequencies. The baseline density measures in this section perform better with raw rather than log frequencies on our evaluation data. Our proposed measures perform significantly better than the baseline measures using both raw and log frequencies.

[2] Goldwater et al. (2010) also consider the number of homophones (words that share a pronunciation with the target word) and frequency-weighted homophones as additional neighborhood measures. In our data there is insufficient homophony for these measures to be significant, so we do not report on experiments using them.

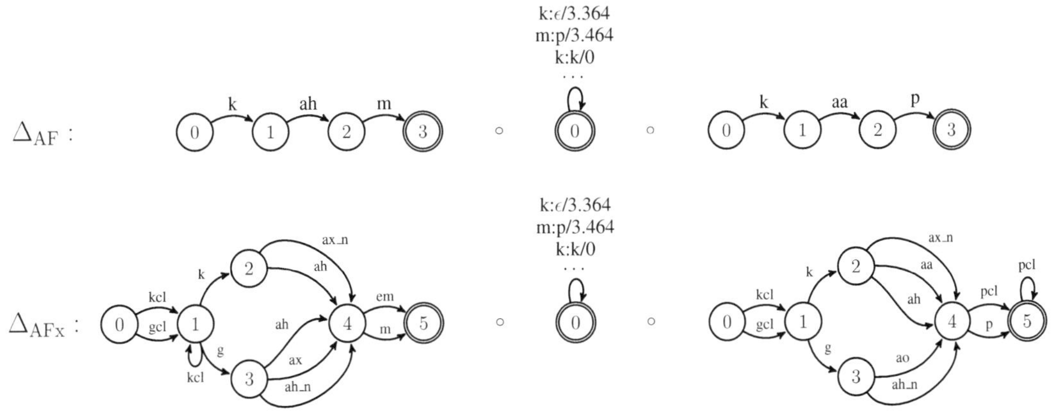

Figure 1: Distance functions implemented using finite-state machines.

the vocal tract variables of articulatory phonology (Browman and Goldstein, 1992), including the constriction degrees and locations of the lips, tongue tip, tongue body, velum and glottis.We borrow a particular feature set from (Livescu, 2005).[3] The substitution cost between two phones is defined as the L1 distance between the articulatory vectors corresponding to the phones. We set the insertion and deletion costs to the mean substitution cost between the articulatory vectors for all phone pairs. These new costs will appear as the arc weights on the edit transducer T. This is shown in Figure 1; apart from the difference in the arc weights on T, Δ_{AF} is the same as Δ_{ED}.

Extended Articulatory Feature-based Edit Distance (Δ_{AFx}): The words in our dictionary are associated with one or more canonical pronunciations written as sequences of phones. The distance functions Δ_{ED} and Δ_{AF} make use of this small set of canonical pronunciations and do not capture the various other ways in which a word can be pronounced. An alternative, explored in some prior work on pronunciation modeling (Deng and Sun, 1994; Richardson et al., 2003; Livescu and Glass, 2004; Mitra et al., 2011; Jyothi et al., 2011), is to model the pronunciation of a word as multiple, possibly asynchronous streams of fine-grained articulatory features, again inspired by articulatory phonology. Such a model can be implemented as a dynamic Bayesian network (DBN) with multiple variables representing the articulatory features in each time frame; please refer to (Livescu and Glass, 2004; Livescu, 2005; Jyothi et al., 2011) for more details. In this approach, deviations from a dictionary pronunciation are the result of either asynchrony between the articulatory streams (accounting for effects such as nasalization, rounding, and epenthetic stops) or the substitution of one articulatory feature value for another (accounting for many reduction phenomena).

Jyothi et al. (2012) describe an approach to encode such a DBN model of pronunciation as an FST that outputs an articulatory feature tuple for each frame of speech. We modify this FST by mapping each articulatory feature tuple to a valid phone as per the phone-to-articulatory-feature mapping used for Δ_{AF} (discarding arcs whose labels do not correspond to a valid phone). The resulting FSTs are used to define Δ_{AFx} by composing with the edit transducer T as in the definition of Δ_{AF}. For computational efficiency, we prune these FSTs to retain only paths that are within three times the weight of the shortest path. The pruned FSTs have hundreds of arcs and $\sim$50 states on average. A schematic diagram is used to illustrate the computation of Δ_{AFx} in Figure 1.

3.2 Weighting Functions

Our weighting functions can be appropriately defined to discount the contributions of words that are infrequent or are very far away. We note here that unlike the density measures in Section 2, the lower the distance-based score for a word (from Equation 1), the more confusable it would be with its neighbors. One approach, as pursued in Nosofsky (1986) and Bailey and Hahn (2001), is to use $\mathrm{score}(w) = \sum_{w'} g(\Delta(w, w'))$ where g is an expo-

[3]The mapping of phones to their articulatory feature values is defined in Appendix B of Livescu (2005). This mapping includes a probability distribution over feature values for certain phones; in these cases, we choose the articulatory feature value with the highest probability.

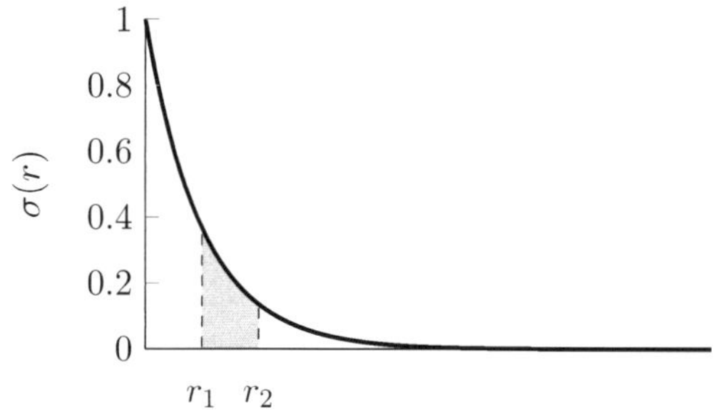

Figure 2: Let w_1 and w_2 be the two closest words to w. The area of the shaded region shows $\beta(w, w_2)$ where $r_i = R_w(w_i) = i$. In the weighted case given in Equation 4, $r_1 = R_w^\eta(w_1)$, $r_2 = R_w^\eta(w_2)$ and $r_2 - r_1 = \eta_w(w_2)$.

nentially decreasing function. This, however, has the disadvantage of being very sensitive to the distance measure used: Slight changes in the distance can alter the score significantly, even if the overall ordering of the distances is preserved. We propose an alternative approach that keeps the score as a linear function of the distances as long as the ordering is fixed. For this, we introduce $\beta(w, w')$ in Equation 1 and let it be a (possibly exponentially) decreasing function of the *rank* of w'.

Formally, we define the rank of w' with respect to w, $R_w(w')$, as follows: Fix an ordering of all $N-1$ words in the vocabulary other than w as $(w_1, w_2, \ldots, w_{N-1})$ such that $\Delta(w, w_i) \leq \Delta(w, w_{i+1})$ for all $i \in \{1, \ldots, N-2\}$. Then $R_w(w') = j$ if $w' = w_j$ in the above ordering. We then define β in terms of a "decay" function σ:

$$\beta(w, w') = \int_{R_w(w')-1}^{R_w(w')} \sigma(r)\mathrm{d}r \qquad (2)$$

If σ is monotonically decreasing, Equation 2 ensures that neighbors with a higher rank (i.e., further away) contribute less weight than neighbors with a lower rank. For example, a measure that gives equal weight to the k closest neighbors (Yarkoni et al., 2008) corresponds to

$$\sigma(r) = \begin{cases} 1 & \text{if } r \leq k \\ 0 & \text{otherwise} \end{cases}$$

Instead of a step function that gives equal weight to all k neighbors, we define σ as an exponentially decreasing function of rank: $\sigma(r) = e^{-r}$. Then, from Equation 2, we obtain $\beta(w, w') = (e-1)e^{-R_w(w')}$. Figure 2 shows the exponentially decreasing $\sigma(r)$ and a sample $\beta(w, w')$.

We know from prior work that it is also important to distinguish among the neighbors depending on how frequently they appear in the language. To account for this, we define a frequency-weighted rank function, $R_w^\eta(w')$:

$$R_w^\eta(w') = \sum_{i=1}^{R_w(w')} \eta_w(w_i) \qquad (3)$$

where η_w is a suitably defined frequency function (see below). We now redefine β as:

$$\beta(w, w') = \int_{R_w^\eta(w')-\eta_w(w')}^{R_w^\eta(w')} \sigma(r)\mathrm{d}r \qquad (4)$$

Note that when $\eta_w(w') = 1$ for all w', Equation 4 reduces to Equation 2. $\beta(w, w')$ is robust in that it is invariant to the ordering used to define rank, R_w^η, i.e. words with the same distance from w can be arbitrarily ordered. Also, multiple words at the same distance contribute to β equally to a single word at the same distance with a frequency that is the sum of their frequencies.

We use three choices for $\eta_w(w')$:

1. The first choice is simply $\eta_w(w') = 1$ for all w'.

2. Let $\pi(w')$ be the unigram probability of w'. We then define $\eta_w(w') = P \cdot \pi(w')$ where P is a scaling parameter. One natural choice for P is the perplexity of the unigram probability distribution, π, i.e., $2^{-\sum_w \pi(w)\log(\pi(w))}$. With this choice of P, when π is a uniform distribution over all words in the vocabulary, we have $\eta_w(w') = 1$ for all w', and $R_w^\eta(w') = R_w(w')$.

3. As defined above, $\eta_w(w')$ does not depend on w. Our third choice for the frequency function considers the frequency of w' relative to w: $\eta_w(w') = \pi(w')/\pi(w)$

To summarize, Equation 1 gives the neighborhood score for w in terms of β and Δ. We use three choices for Δ as specified in Section 3. β is defined by Equation 4 where R_w^η is defined by Equation 3 in terms of the frequency function η_w. We use the three choices described above for η_w. The resulting nine score functions are summarized in Table 1. For completeness, we also include the neighborhood density baseline measures and represent them using our notation with a distance function defined as $\overline{\Delta}_{\mathrm{ND}}(w, w') =$

Measure	$\sigma(r)$	$\Delta(w, w')$	$\eta_w(w')$
ND			1
wND	1	$\overline{\Delta}_{\text{ND}}$	$\pi(w')$
rwND			$\frac{\pi(w')}{\pi(w)}$
ED			1
wED		Δ_{ED}	$\pi(w') \cdot P$
rwED			$\frac{\pi(w')}{\pi(w)}$
AF			1
wAF	e^{-r}	Δ_{AF}	$\pi(w') \cdot P$
rwAF			$\frac{\pi(w')}{\pi(w)}$
AFx			1
wAFx		Δ_{AFx}	$\pi(w') \cdot P$
rwAFx			$\frac{\pi(w')}{\pi(w)}$

Table 1: Summary of neighborhood measures.

$\mathbf{1}(\Delta_{\text{ED}}(w, w') = 1)$ (i.e. $\overline{\Delta}_{\text{ND}}(w, w') = 1$ if $\Delta_{\text{ED}}(w, w') = 1$ and 0 otherwise) and $\sigma = 1$. With $\sigma = 1$ and $\beta(w, w') = \eta_w(w')$, the three choices of η_w give us ND, wND and rwND, as shown in Table 1. The notation $\overline{\Delta}_{\text{ND}}(w, w')$ is to highlight the inverse relationship of the density measures with our distance-based measures.

4 Experiments

We provide an individual analysis of each neighborhood measure as it relates to recognition error rate. We also present a matrix of pairwise comparisons among all of the neighborhood measures with respect to their ability to predict recognition errors. We study the relationship between neighborhood measures and ASR errors in two settings:

- **Isolated-word ASR:** Psycholinguistic studies typically use isolated words as stimuli to study the influence of neighborhood measures on recognition (e.g., see Goldwater et al. (2010) and references therein). Motivated by this, we build an ASR system that recognizes words in isolation and analyze the relationship between its errors and each neighborhood measure. Further details of this analysis are described in Section 4.1.
- **Continuous-word ASR:** ASR systems typically deal with continuous speech. However, the usefulness of neighborhood measures for continuous-word ASR has received little attention, with the notable exception of Goldwater et al. (2010). We further this line of investigation in our second set of experiments by analyzing the relationship between errors made by a continuous-word ASR system and our new measures. These are described in more detail in Section 4.2.

4.1 Isolated-Word ASR

Experimental Setup: We extract isolated words from a subset of the Switchboard-I conversational speech corpus (Godfrey et al., 1992) called the Switchboard Transcription Project, STP (Greenberg et al., 1996; STP, 1996), which is phonetically labeled at a fine-grained level. Isolated words were excised from continuous utterances in sets 20–22 in the STP corpus. We use a total of 401 word tokens (247 unique words) derived from the 3500 most frequent words in Switchboard-I, excluding non-speech events and partial words. These words make up the development and evaluation sets used in prior related work on pronunciation modeling (Livescu and Glass, 2004; Jyothi et al., 2011; Jyothi et al., 2012). We use the dictionary that accompanies the Switchboard-I corpus consisting of 30,241 words; ~98% of these words are associated with a single pronunciation.

The recognition system for this isolated word dataset was built using the Kaldi toolkit (Povey et al., 2011; Kal, 2011). We use an acoustic model that is trained on all of Switchboard-I, excluding the sentences from which our 401-word set was drawn. The ASR system uses standard mel frequency cepstral coefficients with their first and second derivatives (deltas and double-deltas) as acoustic features, with standard normalization and adaptation techniques including cepstral mean and variance normalization and maximum likelihood linear regression. Linear discriminant analysis (LDA) and maximum likelihood linear transform (MLLT) feature-space transformations were applied to reduce the feature-space dimensionality (Povey et al., 2011). The acoustic models are standard Gaussian mixture model-Hidden Markov models (GMM-HMMs) for tied-state triphones. The recognition vocabulary includes 3328 words, consisting of the 3500 most frequent words from Switchboard excluding partial and non-speech words.[4] Since this is an isolated-word task, the ASR system does not use any language model.

Results and Discussion: In order to individually analyze each of the neighborhood measures,

[4]Large-vocabulary automatic recognition of isolated words is a hard task due to the absence of constraints from a language model. Using the entire Switchboard vocabulary would greatly deteriorate the recognition performance on an already hard task. Thus, we restrict the vocabulary to 1/10th of the original size in order to obtain reasonable performance from the isolated ASR system.

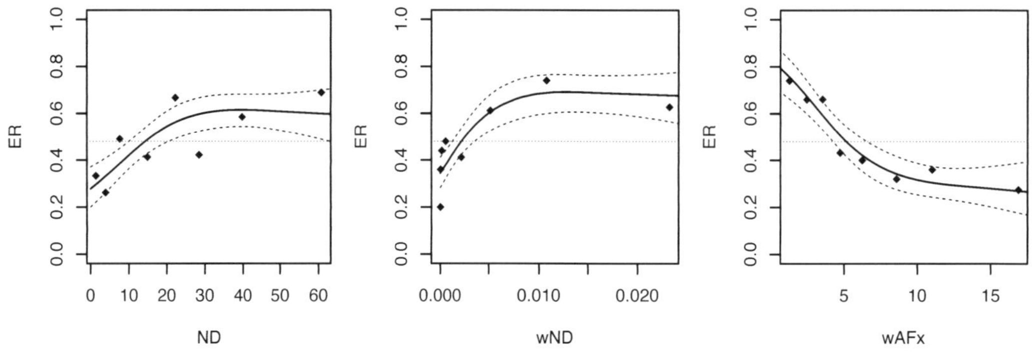

(a) Neighborhood measures ND, wND and wAFx as predictors of isolated-word error rate (ER).

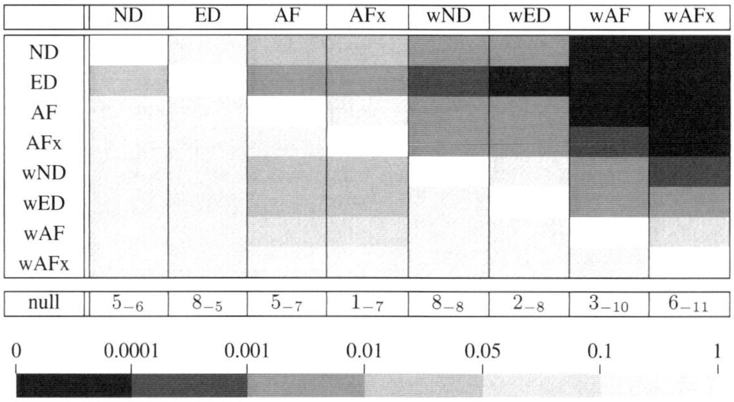

(b) Pairwise comparison of word neighborhood measures as predictors of errors from the isolated-word ASR system using p-values. Many low p-values (darker cells) along a column implies the corresponding measure is a significant predictor of ER.

Figure 3: Analysis of neighborhood measures with isolated word ASR.

following Goldwater et al. (2010), we use a logistic regression model implemented using the *glm* function in R (R Development Core Team, 2005). The logistic regression model fits the log-odds of a binary response variable with a linear combination of one or more predictor variables. For our isolated-word task, the response variable takes a value of either 1 or 0 corresponding to the presence or absence of an error, respectively; we will refer to it as "ER". We build a separate logistic regression model for each neighborhood measure acting as the only predictor of ER. We use restricted cubic splines, using the *rcs* (Harrell Jr., 2012) function in R, to model non-linear predictive relationships. In order to determine whether a neighborhood measure is a significant predictor of ER, we use a likelihood-ratio test (using the *anova* function in R) that compares the fit of the model including only that neighborhood measure as a predictor against the fit of a baseline model including only an intercept and no other predictors. All of the neighborhood measures were found to be significant predictors, with our measures wAF and wAFx being most significant. The p-values from this test are shown in a separate row under the header "null" in Figure 3(b); here, 5_{-6} stands for 5×10^{-6} and so forth. We note that the neighborhood measures are significantly correlated with ER as individual predictors, but classifiers built with each individual measure as the only feature are not good predictors of ASR errors. This is unsurprising as we expect many other predictors other than neighborhood measures, as outlined in Goldwater et al. (2010), to influence ASR errors. This paper focuses only on analyzing each neighborhood measure as an individual predictor; joint models will be explored as part of future work.

Figure 3(a) shows the relationship between errors from the isolated ASR system and three neighborhood measures: the best-performing measure (wAFx) and the two standard density measures (ND, wND). The feature values are aggregated into roughly equal-sized bins and the average error rate for each bin is plotted. The

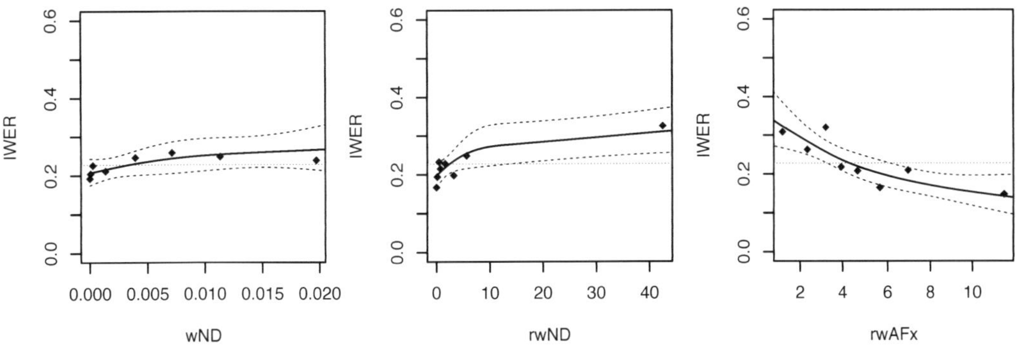

(a) Neighborhood measures wND, rwND and rwAFx as predictors of IWER.

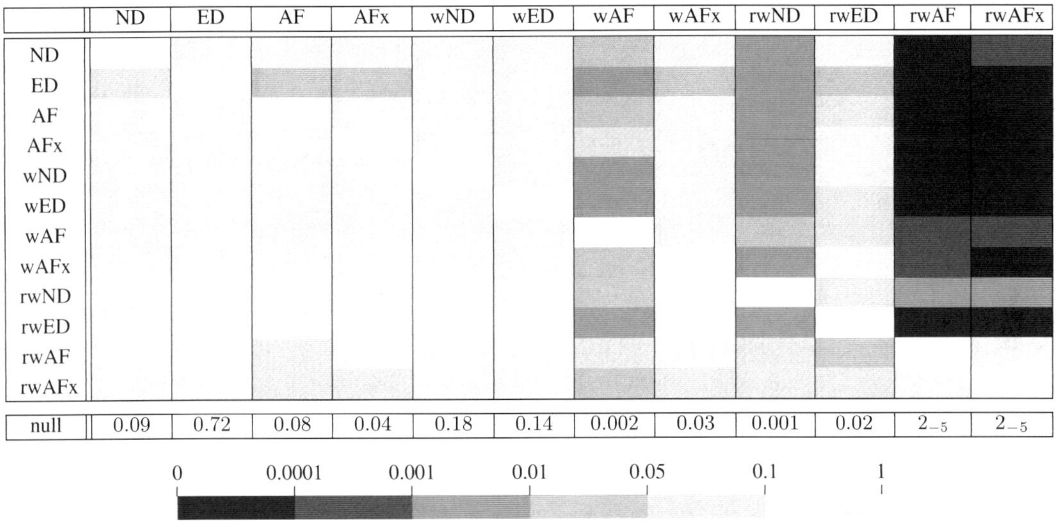

(b) Pairwise comparison of all word neighborhood measures as predictors of IWER from the continuous-word ASR system.

Figure 4: Analysis of neighborhood measures with continuous-word ASR system.

solid line shows the probability of an error from the corresponding logistic regression model and the dashed lines show a 95% confidence interval. The dotted line is the average error rate from the entire data set of 401 words, 0.483. The plots clearly show the inverse relationship between our distance-based measure (wAFx) and the density measures (ND and wND). The slope of the fitted probabilities from the logistic regression model for a measure is indicative of the usefulness of the measure in predicting ER. All of the measures are significant predictors having non-zero slope with a slightly larger slope for wAFx than ND and wND. ND and wND being significant predictors of errors for isolated words is consistent with prior studies from human speech recognition. The proposed measures, wAF and wAFx, stand out as the best predictors of errors. We next analyze the differences between the measures more closely.

Figure 3(b) shows a pairwise comparison of the word neighborhood measures. Each cell $\{i, j\}$ shows a p-value range from a likelihood-ratio test that compares the fit of a logistic regression model using only measure i as a predictor with the fit of a model using both measures i and j as independent predictors. Lower p-values (darker cells) indicate that adding the measure in column j significantly improves the ability of the model to predict ER, as opposed to only using the measure along row i.[5] We use such nested models to compare the model fits using likelihood-ratio significance tests. It is clear from Figure 3(b) that our measures wAF and wAFx are the most significant predictors.

[5]The relative frequency-weighted measures (rwND, rwED, rwAF, rwAFx) were omitted since (wND, wED, wAF, wAFx) are significantly better predictors. This could be because the isolated-word system has no language model and is thus unaffected by the target word frequency.

4.2 Continuous-word ASR

Experimental Setup: For the continuous-word task, our evaluation data consists of full sentences from Switchboard-I that were used to extract the isolated words in Section 4.1. For our analysis, we include all the words in the evaluation sentences that are 3 or more phonemes long and occur 100 times or more in the training set. This gives us a total of 1223 word tokens (459 word types).

The continuous-word ASR system uses an acoustic model trained on all of Switchboard-I excluding the above-mentioned evaluation sentences. The acoustic models are GMM-HMMs for tied-state triphones using MFCC + delta + double-delta features with LDA and MLLT feature-space transformations and speaker adaptation. They are also trained discriminatively using boosted maximum mutual information training from the Kaldi toolkit. We use the entire Switchboard vocabulary of 30,241 words and a 3-gram language model trained on all of the training sentences. The word error rate on the evaluation sentences is 28.3%.[6]

Results and Discussion: Unlike the isolated-word task, the continuous-word ASR system gives word error rates over full utterances. Since we need to measure the errors associated with the individual words, we use the individual word error rate (IWER) metric proposed by Goldwater et al. (2010). The IWER for word w_i is $\alpha \cdot \text{in}_i + \text{del}_i + \text{sub}_i$ where in_i is the number of insertions adjacent to w_i; del_i or sub_i is 1 if w_i is either deleted or substituted, respectively. α is chosen such that $\alpha \cdot \sum_i \text{in}_i = \text{I}$ where I is the total number of insertions for the entire dataset.

As in the isolated-word task, we fit logistic regression models to analyze the neighborhood measures as predictors of IWER. Figure 4(a) shows fitted probabilities from a logistic regression model for IWER built individually using each of the measures wND, rwND and rwAFx as predictors. The number of frequency-weighted neighbors, wND (as well as the number of neighbors, ND), was not found to be a significant predictor of IWER. This is consistent with the findings in Goldwater et al. (2010) that show weak correlations between the number of frequency-weighted neighbors and the probability of misrecognizing a word. However, we find that using the number of frequency-weighted neighbors relative to the frequency of the word (rwND) improves the correlation with the probability of error (seen in Figure 4(a) as an increase in slope). Using our proposed distance measures with relative frequency weighting improves the correlation even further.

Figure 4(b) shows a pairwise comparison of all measures in Table 1; the interpretation is similar to Figure 3(b). We observe that the relative frequency-weighted measures (rwND, rwED, rwAF, rwAFx) are consistently better than their unweighted (ND, ED, AF, AFx) and frequency-weighted (wND, wED, wAF, wAFx) counterparts, with rwAF and rwAFx being most significant. This suggests that the relative frequency-weighted measures are taking precedence in the continuous-word task as significant predictors of IWER (unlike in the isolated-word task) due to the presence of a strong language model.

5 Conclusion

In this work, we propose new word neighborhood measures using distances between words that employ a fine-grained articulatory feature-based representation of the word. We present a new rank-based averaging method to aggregate the word distances into a single neighborhood score. We also suggest multiple ways of incorporating frequency weighting into this score. We analyze the significance of our word neighborhood measures as predictors of errors from an isolated-word ASR system and a continuous-word ASR system. In both cases, our measures perform significantly better than standard neighborhood density measures.

This work reopens the question of whether word neighborhood measures are a useful variable for ASR. There are many possible directions for future work. Our measures could be refined further, for example by exploring alternative distance measures, different articulatory feature sets, different choices of σ and η in the weighting function, or automatically learned costs and distances. Also, our analysis currently looks at each neighborhood measure as an individual predictor; we could jointly analyze the measures to account for possible correlations. Finally, it may be possible to use neighborhood measures in ASR confidence scoring or even directly in recognition as an additional feature in a discriminative model.

[6]The training set includes other utterances from the same speakers in the STP evaluation utterances. This allows for an additional boost in performance from the speaker adapted acoustic models during recognition. Ideally, the training and evaluation sets should not contain utterances from the same speakers. We allow for this to get word error rates that are more comparable to state-of-the-art results on this corpus.

References

T. M. Bailey and U. Hahn. 2001. Determinants of wordlikeness: Phonotactics or lexical neighborhoods? *Journal of Memory and Language*, 44(4):568–591.

C. P. Browman and L. Goldstein. 1992. Articulatory phonology: An overview. *Phonetica*, 49(3-4):155–180.

L. Deng and D.X. Sun. 1994. A statistical approach to automatic speech recognition using the atomic speech units constructed from overlapping articulatory features. *The Journal of the Acoustical Society of America*, 95(5):2702–2719.

E. Fosler-Lussier and N. Morgan. 1999. Effects of speaking rate and word frequency on pronunciations in conversational speech. *Speech Communication*, 29(2):137–158.

E. Fosler-Lussier, I. Amdal, and H-K. J. Kuo. 2005. A framework for predicting speech recognition errors. *Speech Communication*, 46(2):153–170.

J. J. Godfrey, E. C. Holliman, and J. McDaniel. 1992. SWITCHBOARD: Telephone speech corpus for research and development. In *Proc. of ICASSP*.

S. Goldwater, D. Jurafsky, and C. D. Manning. 2010. Which words are hard to recognize? Prosodic, lexical, and disfluency factors that increase speech recognition error rates. *Speech Communication*, 52(3):181–200.

S. Greenberg, J. Hollenback, and D. Ellis. 1996. Insights into spoken language gleaned from phonetic transcription of the Switchboard corpus. In *Proc. of ICSLP*.

U. Hahn and T. M. Bailey. 2005. What makes words sound similar? *Cognition*, 97(3):227–267.

F. E. Harrell Jr. 2012. RMS: Regression Modeling Strategies. R package version 3.5-0.

J. Hirschberg, D. Litman, and M. Swerts. 2004. Prosodic and other cues to speech recognition failures. *Speech Communication*, 43(1):155–175.

P. Jyothi and E. Fosler-Lussier. 2009. A comparison of audio-free speech recognition error prediction methods. In *Proc. of Interspeech*.

P. Jyothi, K. Livescu, and E. Fosler-Lussier. 2011. Lexical access experiments with context-dependent articulatory feature-based models. In *Proc. of ICASSP*.

P. Jyothi, E. Fosler-Lussier, and K. Livescu. 2012. Discriminatively learning factorized finite state pronunciation models from dynamic Bayesian networks. In *Proc. of Interspeech*.

2011. Kaldi. `http://kaldi.sourceforge.net/`.

K. Livescu and J. Glass. 2004. Feature-based pronunciation modeling with trainable asynchrony probabilities. In *Proc. of ICSLP*.

K. Livescu. 2005. Feature-based Pronunciation Modeling for Automatic Speech Recognition. *PhD Dissertation, MIT EECS department*.

P. A. Luce and D. B. Pisoni. 1998. Recognizing spoken words: The neighborhood activation model. *Ear and hearing*, 19:1–36.

P. A. Luce. 1986. Neighborhoods of words in the mental lexicon. *Research on Speech Perception*, (Technical Report No. 6.).

W. D. Marslen-Wilson. 1987. Functional parallelism in spoken word-recognition. *Cognition*, 25(1):71–102.

V. Mitra, H. Nam, C. Y. Espy-Wilson, E. Saltzman, and L. Goldstein. 2011. Articulatory information for noise robust speech recognition. *IEEE Transactions on Audio, Speech, and Language Processing*, 19(7):1913–1924.

R. M. Nosofsky. 1986. Attention, similarity, and the identification–categorization relationship. *Journal of Experimental Psychology: General*, 115(1):39.

D. Povey, A. Ghoshal, et al. 2011. The Kaldi speech recognition toolkit. *Proc. of ASRU*.

R Development Core Team. 2005. R: A language and environment for statistical computing. *R foundation for Statistical Computing*.

M. Richardson, J. Bilmes, and C. Diorio. 2003. Hidden-articulator Markov models for speech recognition. *Speech Communication*, 41(2-3):511–529.

R. A. Scarborough. 2012. Lexical confusability and degree of coarticulation. In *Proceedings of the Annual Meeting of the Berkeley Linguistics Society*.

T. Shinozaki and S. Furui. 2001. Error analysis using decision trees in spontaneous presentation speech recognition. In *Proc. of ASRU*.

1996. The Switchboard Transcription Project. `http://www1.icsi.berkeley.edu/Speech/stp/`.

M. S. Vitevitch and P. A. Luce. 1999. Probabilistic phonotactics and neighborhood activation in spoken word recognition. *Journal of Memory and Language*, 40(3):374–408.

T. Yarkoni, D. Balota, and M. Yap. 2008. Moving beyond Coltheart's N: A new measure of orthographic similarity. *Psychonomic Bulletin & Review*, 15(5):971–979.

The error-driven ranking model of the acquisition of phonotactics: how to keep the faithfulness constraints at bay

Giorgio Magri
SFL (CNRS and University of Paris 8)
UiL OTS (Utrecht University)
magrigrg@gmail.com

Abstract

A problem which arises in the theory of the error-driven ranking model of the acquisition of phonotactics is that the faithfulness constraints need to be promoted but should not be promoted too high. This paper motivates this technical problem and shows how to tune the promotion component of the re-ranking rule so as to keep the faithfulness constraints at bay.

Sections 1-2 introduce the algorithmic framework considered in the paper, namely the *error-driven ranking model* of the acquisition of phonotactics. Section 3 motivates a specific problem which arises in the design and analysis of this model, namely the problem of *controlling* the height reached by the *faithfulness* ($\mathcal{F}$) constraints. Sections 4-6 sketch the theory of $\mathcal{F}$-controlling. Magri (2014a) presents the theory in more detail.

1 The acquisition of phonotactics

Generative linguistics assumes that the learner is provided with a typology of grammars G_1, G_2... The language-learning problem thus consists of individuating the target adult grammar G^* within the typology, on the basis of a finite set of data generated by that grammar. Various formulations of this problem differ for the structural assumptions about the underlying typology, for the type of data fed to the learner, and for the criteria of success used to evaluate the grammar $\hat{G}$ chosen by the learner relative to the target grammar G^*.

In this paper, I focus on the following specific formulation of this general language learning problem. The typology consists of the phonological grammars defined in *Optimality Theoretic* (OT) terms through the rankings of a given set of constraints (Prince and Smolensky, 2004). The data fed to the learner consist of surface forms sampled from the *language* L^* generated by the target OT grammar G^*, namely the set of surface forms which are the phonological realizations of some underlying forms according to G^*. The criteria for success is that the OT grammar $\hat{G}$ chosen by the learner generates a language $\hat{L}$ which coincides with the target one: $\hat{L} = L^*$.

This specific formulation is called the *problem of the acquisition of phonotactics*. In fact, phonotactics is the knowledge of the distinction between licit and illicit forms. Assuming that the distinction is categorical (Gorman, 2013), knowledge of phonotactics reduces to knowledge of the set of licit forms (the set of illicit forms is just the complement). And the set of licit forms relative to an OT grammar G is the corresponding language L_G.

2 The EDRA model

In this paper, I focus on a specific algorithmic approach to the problem of the acquisition of phonotactics, based on *error-driven ranking algorithms* (EDRAs). This approach is summarized below and explained in the rest of this section.

Algorithm 1 *The EDRA model*

Initialize
the ranking values of $\mathcal{F}$ constraints to zero
the ranking values of $\mathcal{M}$ constraints to $\theta^{\text{init}} > 0$
Repeat
1 get a surface form $[y]$ from the target language
2 pick a loser form $[\!z\!]$ (struck through)
3 check whether the current ranking vector $\boldsymbol{\theta}$ is consistent with the underlying/winner/loser form triplet $(/y/, [y], [\!z\!])$ (loser struck through)
4 if it isn't, update the current ranking vector $\boldsymbol{\theta}$
until no more mistakes are made at step 3

The EDRA model maintains a current hypothesis of the target adult grammar, namely a current constraint ranking. This ranking is represented numerically through a *ranking vector* $\boldsymbol{\theta} = (\theta_1, , \theta_n)$

Proceedings of the 2014 Joint Meeting of SIGMORPHON and SIGFSM, pages 10–18,
Baltimore, Maryland USA, June 27 2014. ©2014 Association for Computational Linguistics

which assigns to each constraint C_k a numerical *ranking value* θ_k. A constraint C_k is ranked above another constraint C_h according to a ranking vector $\boldsymbol{\theta}$ provided the ranking value θ_k of the former is (strictly) larger than the ranking value θ_h of the latter (Boersma, 1998; Boersma, 2009).

The current ranking (vector) is initialized in such a way that the corresponding initial language is as small as possible. OT constraints come in two varieties: *faithfulness* ($\mathcal{F}$) and *markedness* ($\mathcal{M}$) constraints. A smallest language corresponds to a ranking which assigns all $\mathcal{F}$ constraints underneath all $\mathcal{M}$ constraints. Thus, the $\mathcal{F}$ constraints are assigned a small initial ranking value, say zero for concreteness; and the $\mathcal{M}$ constraints start with a large positive initial ranking value $\theta^{\text{init}} > 0$. The algorithm then loops through the three steps **1-4**.

At step **1**, the EDRA model receives a piece of data, namely a surface form $[y]$ sampled from the target language L^*. Assuming that the underlying typology satisfies Tesar's (2013) *Surface Orientedness Condition*, this piece of data provides evidence that the target grammar G^* maps this phonological form (construed as the underlying form $/y/$) into itself (construed as the surface form $[y]$) rather than reducing it to some non-faithful candidate $\cancel{[z]}$ (as a mnemonic, I strike out a candidate construed as a loser). In other words, the target adult ranking (vector) $\boldsymbol{\theta}^*$ is *consistent* with the underlying/winner/loser form triplet $(/y/, [y], \cancel{[z]})$ for any loser $\cancel{[z]}$, namely it satisfies condition (1). Here, W (L) is the set of *winner-preferring* (*loser-preferring*) constraints, namely those which assign less (more) violations to the faithful mapping of $/y/$ to $[y]$ than to the neutralization of $/y/$ to $\cancel{[z]}$.

(1) $\max_{C_k \in W} \theta^*_k > \max_{C_h \in L} \theta^*_h$

This consistency condition (1) says that there is at least a winner-preferring constraint which is ranked above all loser-preferring constraints by the target ranking (vector) $\boldsymbol{\theta}^* = (\theta^*_1, \ldots, \theta^*_n)$.

At steps **2** and **3**, the EDRA model thus picks a specific loser $\cancel{[z]}$ and checks whether its current ranking vector $\boldsymbol{\theta}$ satisfies the corresponding consistency condition (1). Failure to satisfy this condition means that the current ranking values of the loser-preferring (winner-preferring) constraints are too large (too small). The algorithm thus promotes the winner-preferring constraints by a small *promotion amount* and demotes the loser-preferring constraints by a small *demotion amount*. What matters is not the actual values of the promotion and demotion amounts, but rather their ratio. Thus, the demotion amount can be set equal to 1 for concreteness, letting instead the promotion amount be equal to an arbitrary nonnegative constant $p \geq 0$, as in (2).

(2) a. Increase the ranking value of each winner-preferring constraint by $p \geq 0$;

b. decrease the ranking value of each *undominated* loser-preferring constraint by 1.

Crucially, not *all* loser-preferring constraints are demoted by (2b), but only those that need to be demoted, namely the *undominated* ones (Tesar and Smolensky, 1998), whose current ranking value is at least as large as the ranking value of all winner-preferring constraints and thus are responsible for flouting the consistency condition (1).

3 The problem of $\mathcal{F}$-control

The crucial implementation parameter of the EDRA model is the promotion amount $p \geq 0$ used in the promotion component (2a) of the re-ranking rule. How should this parameter be tuned so as to optimize the performance of the EDRA model of the acquisition of phonotactics? This section explains how this question leads to the problem of controlling the height of the $\mathcal{F}$ constraints.

3.1 Some initial guarantees

The problem of the acquisition of phonotactics in OT is intractable: no algorithm can solve efficiently an arbitrary instance of the problem corresponding to an arbitrary constraint set (Magri, 2013a). Prompted by this intractability result, Magri (2013b) starts to tackle the problem by looking at a class of "easy" cases.

The intuitive idea is that the relative ranking of the $\mathcal{F}$ constraints might often be irrelevant for phonotactics, namely for drawing the line between licit and illicit forms (although it is of course always crucial for phonology, namely for the specific way in which illicit forms are repaired). This intuition that the relative ranking of the $\mathcal{F}$ constraints is not relevant to describe a certain phonotactic pattern can be formalized as follows. A *partial* constraint ranking is any partial order on the constraint set. A partial ranking *generates* a language provided each one of its total refinements generates that language in the usual OT sense (Yanovich, 2012). A language is called $\mathcal{F}$-*irrelevant* provided it can be generated in this technical sense by a partial ranking which does not rank any two $\mathcal{F}$ constraints relative to each other (see subsection 3.2 for an example).

Suppose that the EDRA model is trained on a target language L^* which is $\mathcal{F}$-irrelevant. The $\mathcal{M}$ constraints start out high, with an initial ranking value θ^{init} usually larger than the number m of markedness constraints. The $\mathcal{F}$ constraints instead start out low, with a null initial ranking value. Throughout learning, the $\mathcal{F}$ constraints will raise, if the algorithm adopts a non-null promotion amount $p > 0$. Theorem 1 provides guarantees that the EDRA model learns the target phonotactics, as long as the $\mathcal{F}$ constraints don't raise too high, namely their ranking values remain smaller by at least m than the initial ranking value θ^{init} of the $\mathcal{M}$ constraints, as stated in (3).

Theorem 1 *Suppose that the underlying OT typology satisfies the following two assumptions. First, if a surface form $[y]$ is a non-faithful candidate of an underlying form $/x/$, then there exists at least one faithfulness constraint which assigns at least one violation to the mapping of $/x/$ into $[y]$ (*$\mathcal{F}$-discernibility assumption*). Second, a form $[y]$ is a candidate of an underlying form $/x/$ if and only if the latter form construed as the surface form $[x]$ is vice versa a candidate of the former form construed as the underlying form $/y/$ (*symmetric candidacy assumption*). Consider a language in this OT typology which is $\mathcal{F}$-irrelevant. Suppose that the EDRA model only makes a finite number of errors and then converges to a final ranking vector which is never updated again. Suppose furthermore that the ranking value θ_F of any $\mathcal{F}$ constraint F at any time in the run satisfies condition (3), where m is the number of $\mathcal{M}$ constraints and $\theta^{init} > m$ their initial ranking value.*

(3) $\boxed{\theta_F \leq \theta^{init} - m}$

Then, the language generated by (an arbitrary refinement of) the final ranking vector learned by the EDRA model coincides with the target language the EDRA model has been trained on. ■

The two assumptions of $\mathcal{F}$-discernibility and symmetric candidacy required by theorem 1 are extremely mild. Magri (2013b; 2014b) conjectures that the relative ranking of the faithfulness constraints turns out to matter for phonotactics only in very special configurations, so that the $\mathcal{F}$-irrelevancy assumption might plausibly hold in the vast majority of cases. Theorem 1 thus provides guarantees that the EDRA model succeeds at the problem of the acquisition of phonotactics in a large class of cases under two crucial assumptions. One assumption is that it can only make a finite number of errors before it *converges* to a final ranking which is consistent with any form and thus never updated. The other assumption is the condition (3) that the height of the $\mathcal{F}$-constraints can be properly controlled.

3.2 Some examples

To illustrate the issues raised by convergence and $\mathcal{F}$-control, consider the following OT typology. The set of forms consists of only four forms $\{apsa, apza, absa, abza\}$. The faithfulness constraints are the two identity constraints for voicing in stops and fricatives (F_1, F_2). The markedness constraints are the two corresponding constraints against stop and fricative voicing (M_1, M_2) plus an additional constraint M which bans sequences of stops and fricatives which agree in voicing, namely it is violated by the two forms *apsa* and *abza*. The candidacy relation is total: the four forms are all candidates of each other.

The OT typology just described contains in particular the language $L = \{$[absa], [apza]$\}$. This language is generated by any ranking which satisfies the ranking conditions (4).

(4)
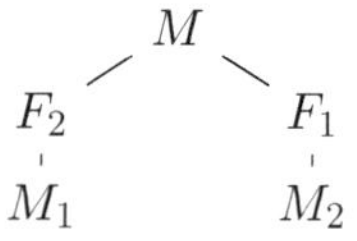

These ranking conditions (4) say nothing about the relative ranking of the two $\mathcal{F}$ constraints F_1 and F_2. The language L thus qualifies as $\mathcal{F}$-irrelevant.

When trained on this language, the EDRA model will be provided at step 1 with a sequence of the two licit forms [absa] and [apza]. It will then complete them into an underlying/winner/loser form triplet at steps 2 and 3 by assuming a faithful underlying form and a non-faithful loser form. The list of all possible such triplets that the algorithm can consider is provided in (5).

(5)

	F_1	F_2	M_1	M_2	M
(/absa/, [absa], ~~[apsa]~~)	W	e	L	e	W
(/absa/, [absa], ~~[abza]~~)	e	W	e	W	W
(/absa/, [absa], ~~[apza]~~)	W	W	L	W	e
(/apza/, [apza], ~~[abza]~~)	W	e	W	e	W
(/apza/, [apza], ~~[apsa]~~)	e	W	e	L	W
(/apza/, [apza], ~~[absa]~~)	W	W	W	L	e

Each triplet is described here in *ERC notation* (Prince, 2002): constraints which are winner- or loser-preferring or even relative to a triplet are marked with a corresponding W or L or e.

The triplets where the constraint M is winner-preferring will trigger virtually no update, since that constraint starts high and is never demoted, and will thus always ensure consistency with those triplets. The learning run is thus driven by the two remaining triplets, boldfaced in (5), which I assume are fed one after the other to the algorithm. Suppose the promotion amount is non-null, say equal to the demotion amount: $p = 1$. The resulting learning run is described in (6).

(6)
$$\begin{matrix} F_1 \\ F_2 \\ M_1 \\ M_2 \\ M \end{matrix} \begin{bmatrix} 0 \\ 0 \\ 5 \\ 5 \\ 5 \end{bmatrix} \rightarrow \begin{bmatrix} 1 \\ 1 \\ 4 \\ 6 \\ 5 \end{bmatrix} \rightarrow \begin{bmatrix} 2 \\ 2 \\ 5 \\ 5 \\ 5 \end{bmatrix} \rightarrow \begin{bmatrix} 3 \\ 3 \\ 4 \\ 6 \\ 5 \end{bmatrix} \rightarrow \begin{bmatrix} 4 \\ 4 \\ 5 \\ 5 \\ 5 \end{bmatrix} \rightarrow \begin{bmatrix} 5 \\ 5 \\ 4 \\ 6 \\ 5 \end{bmatrix} \rightarrow \begin{bmatrix} 6 \\ 6 \\ 5 \\ 5 \\ 5 \end{bmatrix}$$

The two $\mathcal{F}$ constraints end up too high, namely with a final ranking value $\theta_{F_1} = \theta_{F_2} = 6$ which is larger than the initial ranking value $\theta^{\text{init}} = 5$ of the $\mathcal{M}$ constraints. And indeed the EDRA has failed at learning the target phonotactics: since the $\mathcal{F}$ constraints are ranked at the top, the model has incorrectly learned that any form is licit.

A trivial strategy to enforce the $\mathcal{F}$-control condition (3) would be to threshold the promotion component (2a) of the re-ranking rule, as in (2a′).

(2) a′. Increase the ranking value of each winner-preferring constraint by p, *except for an $\mathcal{F}$ constraint which is already close to the forbidden threshold $\theta^{\text{init}} - m$.*

Yet, suppose we tried to remedy to the failure in (6) by thresholding the promotions as in (2a′). When an $\mathcal{F}$ constraint reaches the height $\theta^{\text{init}} - m = 5 - 3 = 2$, we stop promoting it, as boldfaced in the learning run (7).

(7)
$$\begin{matrix} F_1 \\ F_2 \\ M_1 \\ M_2 \\ M \end{matrix} \begin{bmatrix} 0 \\ 0 \\ 5 \\ 5 \\ 5 \end{bmatrix} \rightarrow \begin{bmatrix} 1 \\ 1 \\ 4 \\ 6 \\ 5 \end{bmatrix} \rightarrow \begin{bmatrix} 2 \\ 2 \\ 5 \\ 5 \\ 5 \end{bmatrix} \rightarrow \begin{bmatrix} \mathbf{2} \\ \mathbf{2} \\ 4 \\ 6 \\ 5 \end{bmatrix} \rightarrow \begin{bmatrix} \mathbf{2} \\ \mathbf{2} \\ 5 \\ 5 \\ 5 \end{bmatrix} \rightarrow \begin{bmatrix} \mathbf{2} \\ \mathbf{2} \\ 4 \\ 6 \\ 5 \end{bmatrix} \rightarrow \begin{bmatrix} \mathbf{2} \\ \mathbf{2} \\ 5 \\ 5 \\ 5 \end{bmatrix} \ldots$$

In this run, the constraint M stays put at its initial position. The constraints M_1 and M_2 oscillate up and down, because promoted and demoted by the two boldfaced triplets in (5). The constraints F_1 and F_2 raise a bit until they hit the threshold, and then settle. The EDRA model will thus keep making mistakes forever, without ever converging to a ranking vector consistent with the data.

3.3 Against a null promotion amount

These difficulties with convergence and the $\mathcal{F}$-control condition (3) would disappear if the promotion amount p was set equal to zero, so that the EDRA performs no constraint promotion at all. In fact, Tesar and Smolensky (1998) guarantee convergence for the demotion-only case. And the $\mathcal{F}$ constraints could not possibly be promoted too high, as they would not be promoted at all.

Unfortunately, the option of a null promotion amount is not viable, as argued in Magri (2012; 2014b). In fact, recall that the EDRA model at step **3** always considers underlying/winner/loser form triplets $(/y/, [y], \not{[z]})$ which have an underlying form $/y/$ faithful to the winner $[y]$. This means that the $\mathcal{F}$ constraints are never loser-preferring and are therefore never demoted. If the promotion amount is set equal to zero, then they will not be promoted either. In the end, the $\mathcal{F}$ constraints will thus never be re-ranked. This hampers the ability of the EDRA model to learn the correct relative ranking of the $\mathcal{F}$ constraints when trained on a $\mathcal{F}$-relevant language, namely when it needs to learn a phonotactic pattern which crucially does require a specific relative ranking of the $\mathcal{F}$ constraints.

3.4 Convergence through calibration

As recalled above, Tesar and Smolensky (1998) show that the EDRA model converges when the promotion amount is null and the algorithm performs only constraint demotion. It could in principle be the case that convergence does not extend to the demotion/promotion case, because any amount of promotion disrupts convergence. But Magri (2012) shows that is not the case: convergence extends to EDRAs which perform constraint promotion as well, as long as the promotion amount is small enough. In particular, consider a promotion amount p which scales as in (8) with the numbers ℓ and w of currently undominated loser-preferring constraints and of winner-preferring constraints.

(8) $$p = \frac{\ell}{w + \sigma}$$

It turns out that the EDRA model converges efficiently if (and only if) the promotion amount is *calibrated*, namely has the shape in (8) corresponding to some strictly positive *calibration constant* $\sigma > 0$. The larger the calibration constant σ, the smaller the promotion amount. The case of a null promotion amount corresponds to the limiting case $\sigma = \infty$.

3.5 $\mathcal{F}$-control through calibration as well

Let's take stock. Theorem 1 provides some initial guarantees of success of the EDRA model of the acquisition of phonotactics. These guarantees hold under two crucial assumptions: convergence and the $\mathcal{F}$-control condition (3). Do these assumptions hold when the promotion amount is non-null? Convergence does hold, if the promotion amount, although not null, is nonetheless small, namely calibrated as in (8). What about the $\mathcal{F}$-control condition (3)? Can we play the same trick of a small promotion amount? Or is it the case that, no matter how small the promotion amount, as soon as it is allowed to be non-null, the $\mathcal{F}$ constraints raise too high through a long sequence of very small promotions? Section 4 shows that the latter scenario can never arise: the $\mathcal{F}$ constraints can never raise too high if the promotion amount is small enough. More precisely, it assumes a calibrated promotion amount as in (8). And it shows that the $\mathcal{F}$-control condition (3) holds when the calibration constant σ is large enough, namely it grows as the number m of $\mathcal{M}$ constraints.

As the calibration constant increases as the number m of markedness constraints, the promotion amount decreases quickly. Is it possible to improve on the analysis of section 4 and guarantee the $\mathcal{F}$-control condition (3) with a calibration constant σ which does not grow with the number m of markedness constraints? Unfortunately, section 5 shows that the calibration constant must increase with m. More precisely, this section considers the very simple case where there is a single $\mathcal{F}$ constraint and where the $\mathcal{M}$ constraints are always loser-preferring (or even) but never winner-preferring. In this case, the $\mathcal{F}$-control condition fails if the calibration constant σ does not grow with m at least as $\frac{m}{\log m}$.

Interestingly, the derivative of the function $\frac{m}{\log m}$ goes to zero as m grows. In other words, although the function increases with m, the rate of increase becomes smaller and smaller, making this function as close as possible to a constant. Is this particularly favorable choice of the calibration constant only possible in the peculiar case considered in section 5? or does this favorable choice of the calibration constant ensure $\mathcal{F}$-calibration also in the general case? Section 6 shows how to relax at least one of the two restrictive assumptions made in section 5, namely the assumption that the $\mathcal{M}$ constraints are never winner-preferring.

4 $\mathcal{F}$-controlling with a non-null promotion amount

The most basic question of the theory of $\mathcal{F}$-control is as follows: is it possible to guarantee the $\mathcal{F}$-control condition (3) despite a non-null promotion amount? This section provides a positive answer to this question. In particular, assume the promotion amount p is calibrated as in (8), through the calibration constant σ. The $\mathcal{F}$-control condition then holds provided the calibration constant σ satisfies the bound (9), where m is the number of $\mathcal{M}$ constraints and θ^{init} is their initial ranking value.

(9) $$\sigma \geq \frac{2m + m\theta^{\text{init}}}{\theta^{\text{init}} - m}$$

To get a sense of the bound (9), assume that the initial ranking value θ^{init} of the $\mathcal{M}$ constraints is some power of the number m of $\mathcal{M}$ constraints: $\theta^{\text{init}} = m^k$ for some $k > 1$. The bound (9) thus becomes $\frac{m^k+2}{m^{k-1}-1}$, which is approximately m.

At each update, each of the ℓ currently undominated loser-preferring constraints is demoted by 1 and each of the w winner-preferring constraints is promoted by p. Because of the specific shape (8) of the promotion amount p, the sum of the current ranking values decreases by $\ell - wp = \ell - \frac{w\ell}{w+\sigma} = \frac{\ell\sigma}{w+\sigma}$. And the latter is at least $\frac{\sigma}{w+\sigma}$, as every update requires at least one undominated loser-preferring constraint, namely $\ell \geq 1$. Let α_i be the number of updates triggered by the ith ERC in the run considered up to the time considered (note that there is only a finite number of ERCs relative to a finite number of constraints). Thus, the sum $\sum_k \theta_k$ of the current ranking values has overall decreased by at least $\sum_i \alpha_i \frac{\sigma}{w_i+\sigma}$ relative to the the sum $\sum_k \theta_k^{\text{init}}$ of the initial ranking values, as stated in (10).

(10) $$\sum_k \theta_k \leq \sum_k \theta_k^{\text{init}} - \sum_i \alpha_i \frac{\sigma}{w_i + \sigma}$$

The sum $\sum_k \theta_k^{\text{init}}$ of the initial ranking values can be computed explicitly as in (11), as the m $\mathcal{M}$ constraints start with the initial ranking value θ^{init} while the $\mathcal{F}$ constraints start with a null initial ranking value.

(11) $$\sum_k \theta_k^{\text{init}} = m\,\theta^{\text{init}}$$

The sum $\sum_k \theta_k$ of the current ranking values can be lower bounded as in (12).

$$(12)\quad \sum_k \theta_k \overset{(a)}{=} \sum_F \theta_F + \sum_M \theta_M \overset{(b)}{\geq} 0 + \sum_M \theta_M \overset{(c)}{>} 0 + m(-2) = -2m$$

In step (11a), I have split the sum over all constraints into the sum over the faithfulness and the markedness constraints. In step (11b), I have noted that the ranking value θ_F of any faithfulness constraint F is always at least as large as 0. In fact, the faithfulness constraints start with a null initial ranking value and are never demoted, because the EDRA model always assumes an underlying form faithful to the winner, so that the faithfulness constraints are never loser-preferring. In step (11c), I have noted that the ranking value θ_M of a markedness constraint M can never get smaller than -2. In fact, suppose by contradiction that M managed to be demoted that low. That would imply that some ERC triggers an update that demotes M despite the fact that its current ranking value is strictly smaller than 0. And that is impossible. In fact, at least one faithfulness constraint F must be winner-preferring relative to that ERC, because of the $\mathcal{F}$-discernibility assumption. Furthermore, that constraint F must already dominate M, because F has a non-negative current ranking value while M has a negative current ranking value.

Using the expressions for the sum of the initial and the current ranking values obtained in (11) and (12) respectively, the original inequality (10) yields the bound in (13).

$$(13)\quad \sum_i \alpha_i \frac{1}{w_i + \sigma} < \frac{2m + m\theta^{\text{init}}}{\sigma}$$

The ranking value θ_F of a generic faithfulness constraint F can now be bound as in (14).

$$(14)\quad \theta_F \overset{(a)}{\leq} \sum_i \alpha_i \frac{1}{w_i + \sigma} \overset{(b)}{<} \frac{2m + m\theta^{\text{init}}}{\sigma} \overset{(c)}{\leq} \theta^{\text{init}} - m$$

In step (14a), I have used the fact that the faithfulness constraint F starts with a null initial ranking value and is promoted by $\frac{1}{w_i+\sigma}$ for each one of the α_i updates triggered by the ith ERC, as long as F is winner-preferring relative to that ERC. In step (14b), I have used the bound computed in (13). And in step (14c), I have used the choice (9) of the calibration constant σ.

The bound obtained in (14) guarantees that the generic faithfulness constraint F never raises above the forbidden threshold $\theta^{\text{init}} - m$, thus complying with the $\mathcal{F}$-control condition (3). In other words, we have obtained the following sufficient solution to the problem of $\mathcal{F}$-controlling.

Theorem 2 *Suppose the underlying typology satisfies the $\mathcal{F}$-discernibility assumption. Consider a run of the EDRA model on an arbitrary language in that typology. Assume that the $\mathcal{F}$ constraints start out with a null initial ranking value while the m $\mathcal{M}$ constraints start out with an initial ranking value $\theta^{\text{init}} > m$. Assume furthermore that the promotion amount is calibrated as in (8) and that the calibration constant σ is large enough to satisfy the bound (9). Then, the ranking values of the $\mathcal{F}$ constraints remain smaller than the forbidden threshold $\theta^{\text{init}} - m$ throughout the entire run.* ■

5 $\mathcal{F}$-controlling on the diagonal case

The preceding section has established the $\mathcal{F}$-control condition (3) when the promotion amount is not null, provided it is small enough, namely it corresponds to a calibration constant which grows as the number m of $\mathcal{M}$ constraints. Is it possible to do better? In particular, is it possible to guarantee $\mathcal{F}$-control when the calibration constant does not increase with m? This section sketches a counterexample which provides a negative answer to this question; see Magri (2014a) for details.

At every iteration, the EDRA model receives a winner form sampled from the target language, assumes a corresponding faithful underlying form and picks a corresponding loser candidate. At every iteration, the model thus constructs an underlying/winner/loser form triplet, which can be described in terms of the corresponding ERC, as exemplified in (5) above. Since there are only a finite number of ERCs corresponding to a finite number of constraints, the ERCs considered in a run of the model can be stacked one on top of the other into an *input ERC matrix*.

Without loss of generality, assume that each input ERC has a unique loser-preferring constraint. Next, let me make two crucial assumptions. First, assume that the constraint set contains a single faithfulness constraint F – plus of course a certain number m of markedness constraints $M_1, \ldots, M_m$. Second, assume that $M_1, \ldots, M_m$

Figure 1: First three stages of the learning dynamics where each diagonal ERC is fed persistently in turn

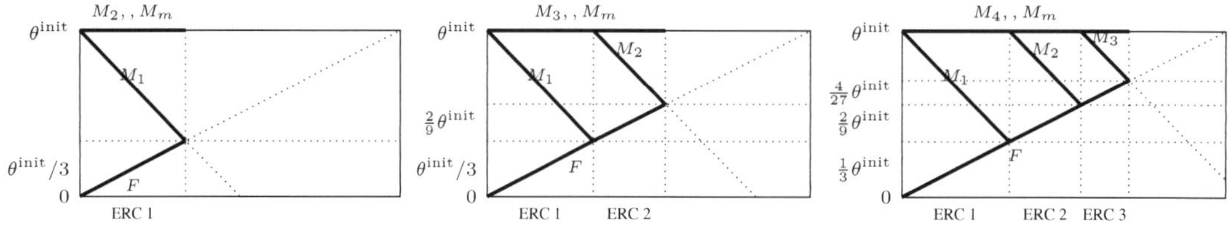

are either loser-preferring or even in the input ERCs, but never winner-preferring. The input ERC matrix thus is (a subset of) the matrix (15).

(15)
$$\begin{array}{r|c|ccc|} & F & M_1 & \ldots & M_m \\ \text{ERC } 1 & \text{W} & \text{L} & & e \\ \vdots & | & & \ddots & \\ \text{ERC } m & \text{W} & e & & \text{L} \end{array}$$

The column corresponding to F consists of all W's. The entries corresponding to $M_1, \ldots, M_m$ are all equal to e's but for the diagonal of L's. This ERC matrix is thus called *diagonal.*

What is the maximum height that the constraint F can reach in a run of the EDRA model on the input diagonal ERC matrix (15)? To address this question, consider the following special run. To start, we persistently feed ERC 1 to the algorithm, until the markedness constraint M_1 is demoted underneath the faithfulness constraint F and that ERC cannot trigger any further update. Only at that point, we stop feeding ERC 1 to the algorithm, and persistently feed ERC 2 instead, again until it cannot trigger any further update. Only at that point, we stop feeding ERC 2 and persistently feed ERC 3. And so on.

Assume that the promotion amount has the shape (8) and suppose for concreteness that the calibration constant is $\sigma = 1$, so that the faithfulness constraint is promoted by $1/2$ with each update. The dynamics of the ranking values is depicted in Figure 1 for the first three learning stages. Throughout stage 1, it is ERC 1 that triggers updates, whereby the markedness constraint M_1 is demoted and the faithfulness constraint is promoted by $\frac{1}{3}\theta = \frac{1}{2+\sigma}\theta^{\text{init}}$, until the two constraints meet. Throughout stage 2, it is ERC 2 that triggers updates, whereby the markedness constraint M_2 is demoted and the faithfulness constraint is promoted by another $\frac{2}{9}\theta = \frac{1+\sigma}{(2+\sigma)^2}\theta^{\text{init}}$, until the two constraints meet. Throughout the generic kth stage, it is the kth ERC that triggers updates, whereby the markedness constraint M_k is demoted and the faithfulness constraint promoted by an amount that turns out to be equal to $\frac{(1+\sigma)^{k-1}}{(2+\sigma)^k}\theta^{\text{init}}$. The height θ_F reached by the faithfulness constraint at the end of the special run considered is thus $\sum_{k=1}^{m} \frac{(1+\sigma)^{k-1}}{(2+\sigma)^k}\theta^{\text{init}}$. It turns out that this is indeed the maximum height reacheable by the faithfulness constraint F on *any* run on the diagonal ERC matrix (15).

The $\mathcal{F}$-control condition (3) thus boils down to the inequality $\sum_{k=1}^{m} \frac{(1+\sigma)^{k-1}}{(2+\sigma)^k}\theta^{\text{init}} \leq \theta^{\text{init}} - m$. Assume that the m markedness constraints start out with the initial ranking value $\theta^{\text{init}} = m^k$. This inequality can then be solved analytically yielding $\sigma(m) = (1 - \exp\{(-k \log m)/m\})^{-1}$. By a first order Taylor expansion $exp(x) \sim 1 + x + o(x^2)$ of the exponential function, the latter expression can be approximated as in (16).

(16) $$\sigma = \sigma(m) \sim \frac{m}{k \log m}$$

The latter bound for the calibration threshold is substantially smaller than the linear bound $\sigma(m) \sim m$ obtained through the elementary analysis of section 6. In particular, although (16) is not bounded as a function of m, its derivative goes to zero as $1/\log m$.

6 $\mathcal{F}$-controlling when the promotion amount decreases *slowly*

The preceding section has made two restrictive assumptions. First, that there is a unique $\mathcal{F}$ constraint. Second, that the $\mathcal{M}$ constraints are never winner-preferring. Under these assumptions, it has shown that the $\mathcal{F}$-control condition (3) holds when the calibration constant grows only very slowly with m, namely as in (16). Does this favorable result also hold when we relax the two restrictive assumptions? This section shows how to relax one of the two assumptions, namely the assumption that the $\mathcal{M}$ constraints cannot be winner-preferring. At this stage, I do know how to relax the other assumption that there is a unique $\mathcal{F}$ constraint. Again, the reasoning here is only sketched; see Magri (2014a) for details.

To illustrate the core idea, suppose that the EDRA model is trained on the input ERC matrix (17a) and walks through the run (18a). Here, I am assuming that the promotion amount p has the shape in (8), with the calibration constant $\sigma = 0$ set equal to zero for concreteness.

(17) a.
$$\begin{array}{r} \\ \text{ERC 1} \\ \text{ERC 2} \end{array} \begin{array}{c} F \quad M_1 \; M_2 \\ \left[\begin{array}{c|cc} \text{W} & \text{L} & e \\ \text{W} & \text{W} & \text{L} \end{array}\right] \end{array}$$

b.
$$\begin{array}{r} \\ \text{ERC 1} \\ \text{ERC 2} \end{array} \begin{array}{c} F \quad M_1 \; M_2 \\ \left[\begin{array}{c|cc} \text{W} & \text{L} & e \\ \text{W} & e & \text{L} \end{array}\right] \end{array}$$

(18) a.
$$\begin{array}{r} F \\ M_1 \\ M_2 \end{array} \begin{bmatrix} 0 \\ 10 \\ 10 \end{bmatrix} \xrightarrow{\text{ERC 1}} \begin{bmatrix} 1 \\ 9 \\ 10 \end{bmatrix} \xrightarrow{\text{ERC 1}} \begin{bmatrix} 2 \\ 8 \\ 10 \end{bmatrix} \xrightarrow{\text{ERC 2}} \begin{bmatrix} 2.5 \\ 8.5 \\ 9 \end{bmatrix} \xrightarrow{\text{ERC 2}} \begin{bmatrix} 3 \\ 9 \\ 8 \end{bmatrix}$$

b.
$$\begin{array}{r} F \\ M_1 \\ M_2 \end{array} \begin{bmatrix} 0 \\ 10 \\ 10 \end{bmatrix} \xrightarrow{\text{ERC 1}} \begin{bmatrix} 1 \\ 9 \\ 10 \end{bmatrix} \xrightarrow{\qquad\text{ERC 2}\qquad} \begin{bmatrix} 2 \\ 9 \\ 9 \end{bmatrix} \xrightarrow{\text{ERC 2}} \begin{bmatrix} 3 \\ 9 \\ 8 \end{bmatrix}$$

Consider the diagonal ERC matrix (17b) corresponding to $m = 2$ markedness constraints. The original run (18a) on the original ERC matrix (17a) can be simulated with the run (18b) on the diagonal ERC matrix (17b) in such a way that all constraints end up at the same high in the two runs.

This reasoning holds in complete generality. Indeed, under the assumption that there is a unique $\mathcal{F}$ constraint but no restrictions on the $\mathcal{M}$ constraints, the input ERC matrix looks like (19).

(19)
$$\begin{array}{c} F_1 \quad M_1 \quad \ldots \quad M_m \\ \left[\begin{array}{c|ccc} | & \ddots & & \cdot^{\cdot^{\cdot}} \\ \text{W} & & \text{L}, e, \text{W} & \\ | & \cdot^{\cdot^{\cdot}} & & \ddots \end{array}\right] \end{array}$$

Any run of the EDRA model on this input ERC matrix (19) can be mimicked by a corresponding run on the diagonal ERC matrix (15). This reduction to the diagonal case holds provided the promotion amount is calibrated, namely has the shape in (8), no matter the choice of the calibration constant $\sigma \geq 0$. This reduction fails if the promotion amount is not calibrated.

Another crucial condition needed for the reduction to the diagonal case is the following: in the original run, the markedness constraints are allowed to raise only slightly above their initial ranking value θ^{init}. Indeed, if a markedness constraint could raise arbitrarily high above its initial ranking value in the original run, there would be no way to mimic that increasing ranking dynamics with a derived run on the diagonal ERC matrix (15), as the latter only demotes but never promotes the markedness constraints. The fact that the markedness constraints can raise by a small amount does not threaten the reduction to the diagonal case, because the markedness constraints can be assigned a slightly larger initial ranking value in the derived run on the diagonal ERC matrix.

Fortunately, the markedness constraints $M_1, \ldots, M_m$ indeed can raise above their initial ranking value θ^{init} only by a small amount, namely never by more than m, as stated in (20).

(20) $\theta_1, \ldots, \theta_m \leq \theta^{\text{init}} + m$

Obviously, this bound (20) holds at the beginning of the run. It is thus sufficient to prove that this bound is an *invariant* of the algorithm: if it holds of the current ranking values at some time $t-1$, then it also holds at the subsequent time t. The challenge is that a winner-preferring markedness constraint M_1 sitting right at $\theta^{\text{init}} + m$ at time $t-1$ could in principle be promoted above that forbidden threshold, so that the bound (20) would hold at time $t-1$ but fail at time t. Yet, in order for such an update to happen, there has got to exist another constraint M_2 which is loser-preferring and is ranked at time $t-1$ at least as high as the winer-preferring constraint M_1. This means in turn that the sum $\theta_1^{t-1} + \theta_2^{t-1}$ of the two ranking values of M_1 and M_2 at time $t-1$ is at least $(\theta^{\text{init}} + m) + (\theta^{\text{init}} + m)$. This suggests to cope with the difficulty just highlighted by strengthening the invariant. Not only a *single* ranking value cannot get larger than $\theta^{\text{init}} + m$, but also the sum of any two ranking values can never reach $(\theta^{\text{init}} + m) + (\theta^{\text{init}} + m)$. For instance, let's say it can never get larger than $(\theta^{\text{init}} + m) + (\theta^{\text{init}} + m - 1)$. But now again, in order to prove that the latter bound on the sum of *two* ranking values holds at time t, I need an assumption about the sum of *three* ranking values at time $t-1$. And so on. Indeed, the sum $\theta_{i_1} + \ldots + \theta_{i_k}$ of the current ranking values of any number k of different markedness constraints $M_{i_1}, \ldots, M_{i_k}$ can be bound as in (21). This bound holds for any promotion amount with the shape (8) corresponding to a calibration constant σ which is not too small, namely $\sigma \geq 1$.

(21) $$\sum_{h=1}^{k} \theta_{i_h} \leq \sum_{h=1}^{k} (\theta^{\text{init}} + m - h + 1)$$

For $k = 1$, (21) yields the desired bound (20).

Acknowledgments

This research was supported by a Marie Curie Intra European Fellowship within the 7th European

Community Framework Programme.

References

Paul Boersma. 1998. *Functional Phonology*. Ph.D. thesis, University of Amsterdam, The Netherlands. The Hague: Holland Academic Graphics.

Paul Boersma. 2009. Some correct error-driven versions of the constraint demotion algorithm. *Linguistic Inquiry*, 40:667–686.

Kyle Gorman. 2013. *Generative phonotactics*. Ph.D. thesis, University of Pennsylvania.

Giorgio Magri. 2012. Convergence of error-driven ranking algorithms. *Phonology*, 29(2):213–269.

Giorgio Magri. 2013a. The complexity of learning in OT and its implications for the acquisition of phonotactics. *Linguistic Inquiry*, 44.3:433468.

Giorgio Magri. 2013b. An initial result on the restrictiveness of the error-driven ranking model of the early stage of the acquisition of phonotactics. In Hsin-Lun Huang, Ethan Poole, and Amanda Rysling, editors, *Proceedings of NELS 43: the 43rd annual meeting of the North East Linguistic Society*.

Giorgio Magri. 2014a. The error-driven ranking model of the acquisition of phonotactics: how to control the height of the faithfulness constraints. CNRS, UiL-OTS ms.

Giorgio Magri. 2014b. Error-driven versus batch models of the acquisition of phonotactics: David defeats Goliath. In John Kingston, Claire Moore-Cantwell, Joe Pater, and Robert Staubs, editors, *Supplemental Proceedings of Phonology 2013*, Washington DC. Linguistic Society of America.

Joe Pater. 2009. Weighted constraints in Generative Linguistics. *Cognitive Science*, 33:999–1035.

Alan Prince and Paul Smolensky. 2004. *Optimality Theory: Constraint Interaction in generative grammar*. Blackwell, Oxford. As Technical Report CU-CS-696-93, Department of Computer Science, University of Colorado at Boulder, and Technical Report TR-2, Rutgers Center for Cognitive Science, Rutgers University, New Brunswick, NJ, April 1993. Also available as ROA 537 version.

Alan Prince. 2002. Entailed ranking arguments. Ms., Rutgers University, New Brunswick, NJ. Rutgers Optimality Archive, ROA 500. Available at http://www.roa.rutgers.edu.

Bruce Tesar and Paul Smolensky. 1998. Learnability in Optimality Theory. *Linguistic Inquiry*, 29:229–268.

Bruce Tesar. 2013. *Output-Driven Phonology: Theory and Learning*. Cambridge Studies in Linguistics.

Igor Yanovich. 2012. The logic of OT rankings. MIT manuscript.

Comparing Models of Phonotactics for Word Segmentation

Natalie M. Schrimpf
Department of Linguistics
Yale University
natalie.schrimpf@yale.edu

Gaja Jarosz
Department of Linguistics
Yale University
gaja.jarosz@yale.edu

Abstract

Developmental research indicates that infants use low-level statistical regularities, or phonotactics, to segment words from continuous speech. In this paper, we present a segmentation framework that enables the direct comparison of different phonotactic models for segmentation. We compare a model using phoneme transitional probabilities, which have been widely used in computational models, to syllable-based bigram models, which have played a prominent role in the developmental literature. We also introduce a novel estimation method, and compare it to other strategies for estimating the parameters of the phonotactic models from unsegmented data. The results show that syllable-based models outperform the phoneme models, specifically in the context of improved unsupervised parameter estimation. The syllable-based transitional probability model achieves a word token f-score of nearly 80%, the highest reported performance for a phonotactic segmentation model with no lexicon.

1 Introduction

One of the first language learning tasks infants must solve is the segmentation of fluent speech into words. Extensive experimental work has demonstrated that infants are able to use phonotactic restrictions (Jusczyk & Luce, 1994; Mattys et al., 1999; Mattys & Jusczyk, 2001) and other low-level statistical regularities (Saffran et al., 1996; Thiessen & Saffran, 2003; Pelucchi et al., 2009) to extract words from fluent speech before the age of one. This work has shown that infants utilize these low-level statistical regularities to segment speech during the second half of the first year of life before they have developed extensive vocabularies that could provide top-down lexical information to guide segmentation. Developmental research indicates that on average infants know fewer than 100 word types during this period (Dale & Fenson, 1996; Daland & Pierrehumbert, 2011).

One statistical cue that has received a great deal of support in experimental work on infant speech segmentation is transitional probability calculated over syllables. In foundational work, Saffran et al. (1996) found that infants are able to segment words from continuous speech using statistical regularities between syllables. Numerous subsequent studies have confirmed that infants can track transitional probabilities and use them to segment speech (Aslin et al., 1998; Thiessen & Saffran, 2003; Pelucchi et al., 2009).

Despite the extensive experimental literature demonstrating infants' sensitivity to transitional probability in an artificial language learning setting, the utility of these statistical cues in a natural language learning context is disputed. Yang (2004) shows that a segmentation strategy relying on transitional probabilities over syllables achieves very poor results on English child-directed speech, even when the input is perfectly syllabified. Yang implements the local minimum segmentation strategy proposed by Saffran et al. (1996) wherein word boundaries are posited at syllable transitions whenever the transitional probabilities at these positions are lower than at the neighboring transitions. He reports that this strategy discovers a mere 23% of target words and posits incorrect words nearly 60% of the time. Swingley (2005) argues that statistical cues calculated over syllables can provide sufficient information for infants to begin building an initial lexicon. However, the learning strategy explored by Swingley is highly conservative, reliably detecting only a small proportion of target words in the input. Overall, these results raise questions about whether syllable-based statistics can be reliably used to identify word boundaries in natural language data.

Proceedings of the 2014 Joint Meeting of SIGMORPHON and SIGFSM, pages 19–28,
Baltimore, Maryland USA, June 27 2014.

While the experimental work emphasizes syllable-level transitional probability, recent computational modeling work and corpus analyses have primarily focused on the utility of phoneme-level statistics. A number of phonotactically-based segmentation models, focusing on the discovery of word boundaries based on phoneme-level statistics, have achieved more promising results (Adriaans & Kager, 2010; Daland & Pierrehumbert, 2011; see also Brent, 1999). For example, Brent (1999) showed that a local minimum strategy relying on phoneme bigrams correctly extracts about 50% of word tokens in English child-directed speech. Corpus analyses of child-directed speech have also highlighted the information content of phoneme-level statistics (Hockema, 2006; Jarosz & Johnson, 2013). Related work has shown that phonotactic information can improve the performance of state-of-the-art segmentation models whose primary objective is to discover the lexicon that underlies the regularities in the continuous speech signal. Again, this work has largely emphasized phoneme-level statistical cues (Blanchard & Heinz 2008, 2010), and those models that do rely on syllable structure (Johnson, 2008a; Johnson & Goldwater, 2009), do not directly encode sequential statistics between adjacent syllables of the sort investigated in the infant literature. Finally, some models assume computations are performed over syllables and that all word boundaries in the input are aligned with syllable boundaries, but provide no mechanism by which such language-specific syllabification principles could be learned (Yang, 2004; Swingley, 2005; Lignos & Yang, 2010).

Overall, the existing evidence clearly shows that there are phonotactic cues to word boundaries in spontaneous, child-directed speech. However, there are remaining questions regarding the exact nature of these cues, their reliability, and how they relate to the statistical cues explored in the infant word segmentation literature. In this paper, we investigate the computational mechanisms underlying infants' early speech segmentation abilities relying on low-level statistical regularities, or phonotactics. We present a computational framework that permits the direct comparison of segmentation predictions for alternative models of phonotactics. In particular, we compare a standard phonotactic model relying on phoneme-level bigrams to two syllable-based phonotactic models relying on transitional probabilities. Unlike previous models relying on syllabified data (Yang, 2004; Swingley, 2005; Lignos & Yang, 2010), we do not assume that word boundaries align with syllable boundaries in the input. Rather, we present a simple syllabification method that can be used to model phonotactic probability for arbitrary strings using statistics estimated from unsyllabified, unsegmented utterances. We also compare the local minimum segmentation strategy (Saffran et al., 1996; Yang, 2004) to alternatives designed to deal with the challenges of unsupervised estimation of transitional probabilities from unsegmented input.

Our focus on the early phonotactic segmentation stage differentiates our approach from many computational models emphasizing the discovery of the lexicon and higher-level language structure (Brent, 1999; Venkataraman, 2001; Swingley, 2005; Johnson, 2008a; Goldwater et al., 2009; Johnson & Goldwater, 2009; Blanchard & Heinz 2008, 2010; Lignos & Yang, 2010). It complements that of recent work investigating the use of phoneme-level statistical regularities for segmentation (Adriaans & Kager, 2010; Daland & Pierrehumbert, 2011). Our work differs from these latter approaches, however, in comparing several phonotactic models, including ones relying on the syllable-based transitional probability statistics investigated in infant research. Our work also contributes to existing segmentation work that assumes a syllabified input (Yang, 2004; Swingley, 2005; Lignos & Yang, 2010) by showing how many aspects of syllable structure can be inferred.

Our results reveal an interaction between estimation strategy and the choice of phonotactic model. The local minimum segmentation strategy works poorly in general for all models considered, but the lowest performance is achieved by the syllable-based models. However, when the same cues are used in the context of a simple, generative probability model with improved unsupervised parameter estimation, the syllable-based models substantially outperform the phoneme-based models. Indeed, the syllable-based transitional probability phonotactic model achieves a word token segmentation f-score of nearly 80%, which is the highest reported performance among purely phonotactically-based segmentation models (Adriaans & Kager, 2010; Daland & Pierrehumbert, 2011). Indeed, this performance compares favorably with state-of-the-art segmentation models that involve learning of higher level regularities, such as the lexicon and collocations (Brent, 1999; Venkataraman, 2001; Johnson, 2008a; Goldwater et al., 2009; Johnson & Goldwater, 2009), and demonstrates that good segmentation performance can be achieved by exploiting simple syllable-level phonotactic cues.

2 Segmentation Model

The proposed segmentation model defines the probability of an utterance in terms of an abstract phonotactic probability component that assigns word well-formedness probabilities to phoneme strings. The segmentation algorithm uses those probabilities to determine the maximum likelihood segmentation as defined by a simple generative model. Since the phonotactics and segmentation components are separate, they can be independently modified. This framework makes it possible to compare models of phonotactics while using the same segmentation strategy.

2.1 Probability Model

The segmentation probability model relies on the phonotactic component to assign probabilities to potential words. The probability of a segmentation *w* is defined in terms of a simple unigram model by multiplying the probabilities of the words $w_{1...n}$ posited in that segmentation.

1) $P(w) = P(w_{1...n}) = \prod_1^n P(w_i)$

$P(w_i)$ is the probability assigned by the phonotactic models, which will be defined in the next section. The various phonotactic models change how exactly $P(w_i)$ is defined, but the segmentation probability always depends directly on the word probabilities given by a particular phonotactic model. For example, for the utterance [lʊkætmi] 'lookatme', the segmentation model compares different segmentations, such as [lʊk#æ#tmi] and [lʊk#æt#mi] based on the phonotactic well-formedness of the posited words.

2.2 Segmentation Algorithm

The segmentation algorithm computes and outputs the segmentation with the highest likelihood: $argmax_w P(w)$. The optimal segmentation is found using dynamic programming, as in several previous proposals (Brent, 1999; Venkataraman, 2001). Given an input utterance, the model considers placing word boundaries at different positions within the utterance without regard to phonotactics or syllable structure. The phonotactic probability of each posited word is calculated independently as it is considered and used to update the probability of segmentations utilizing that word. In this way, the segmentation component remains entirely divorced from the details of the phonotactic models. Crucially, this means the full space of possible segmentations is considered by the segmentation model regardless of the phonotactic model, with no a priori restrictions imposed by phonotactic or syllable constraints as to where boundaries are permitted.

3 Phonotactic Models

We implement and compare several models of phonotactics that are utilized by the segmentation component described above. While all models rely on transitional probabilities, or bigrams, as defined in (2), the unit of analysis varies between the models. One model uses phonemes and phoneme transitions, and two models incorporate syllable information: we use *x* to denote a generic unit. The model determines the probability of a word, $w = x_{0...n+1}$ where x_0 and x_{n+1} are the word boundary symbol #, by multiplying the probabilities of all bigrams in the word.

2) $P(w) = \prod_0^n P(x_{i+1}|x_i)$

The transitional probability for the sequence $x_i x_{i+1}$ can be calculated using relative frequency estimates based on counts C in the corpus.

3) $\hat{P}(x_i|x_{i-1}) = \frac{C(x_{i-1}x_i)}{C(x_{i-1})}$

Section 4 describes strategies that we consider for estimating these parameters in an unsupervised way from unsegmented data where the only word boundaries are those that coincide with utterance boundaries.

3.1 Phoneme Model

The first phonotactic model is a standard phoneme bigram model that determines the probability of a word by multiplying the phoneme bigrams in the word (Jurafsky & Martin, 2008). For example, to calculate the phonotactic probability of the sequence [bot] as a word, this model multiplies together P(b|#)P(o|b)P(t|o)P(#|t).

3.2 Syllable-Based Models

The other two phonotactic models use syllables rather than phonemes. One model relies on transitional probabilities over syllables, and the other uses onsets and rhymes as the unit of analysis.

3.2.1 Unsupervised Syllabification

The syllabification method relies on the language universal principle of onset maximization together with an inventory of syllable onsets derived from the beginnings of utterances. When syllabifying an intervocalic sequence of consonants, this method finds the longest legal onset aligned with the right edge and places any remaining consonants in the coda of the previous syllable. Thus, a sequence like [ætmi] would be syllabified as [æt.mi] in English since [m] but not [tm] occurs utterance-initially. The only language-particular information required for this approach is knowledge of which phonemes are vowels (syllabic) and which are consonants, a limited type of information also assumed by other syllable inference models for segmentation (Johnson, 2008a; Johnson & Goldwater, 2009).

As the segmentation component posits potential words, they are passed to the phonotactic component for syllabification and phonotactic probability calculation. This differs crucially from previous work assuming a fixed syllabification of the input corpus in which word boundaries always align with syllable boundaries (Yang, 2004; Swingley, 2005; Lignos & Yang, 2010). In a setting in which syllabification must be inferred from unsegmented utterances, the learner must be capable of assigning syllabification more flexibly since word boundaries do not always align with the syllable boundaries that would be posited for the utterance as a whole. For example, the universal onset maximization principle always parses singleton consonants VCV as the onsets V.CV rather than codas VC.V. Therefore, without prior knowledge of word boundaries, the utterance [lʊkætmi] ('look at me') would be syllabified as [lʊ.kæt.mi], and if the segmentation algorithm never considered words that misaligned with these syllable boundaries, it would never extract any vowel-initial words like 'at'. Thus, a crucial feature of the current model is that syllabification takes place on a word-by-word basis as potential words are posited. The resulting syllabification for the potential word is used by the syllable-based models to assign phonotactic probability as discussed below.

3.2.2 Syllable Model

The first syllable-based model is one in which bigram transitional probabilities are calculated over syllables. These transitional probabilities are precisely those discussed earlier as having played a prominent role in the infant segmentation literature. The phonotactic probability of a posited word is calculated by multiplying the transitional probabilities of all syllable bigrams in the word, including an assumed initial and final #. For example, if the segmentation component posits a potential word such as [lʊkætmi] 'lookatme', this sequence is first syllabified using the procedure described earlier as [lʊ.kæt.mi]. Then the phonotactic probability of this potential word is calculated by multiplying together the syllable-based bigram probabilities: P(lʊ|#)P(kæt|lʊ)P(mi|kæt)P(#|mi). As before, relative frequency estimates calculated from unsegmented input data (automatically syllabified using the unsupervised syllabification method described earlier) provide a starting point for parameter estimation. Estimation strategies are discussed in depth in Section 4.

3.2.3 Onset Rhyme Model

In addition to the phoneme level and syllable level bigram models, we consider an intermediate model that makes use of the main subconstituents of syllables: onsets and rhymes. Recall that the syllabification procedure relies on identifying maximal onsets, whereas rhymes are composed of the remaining material in the syllable. So these constituents are already available during the syllabification procedure, and this phonotactic model operates over these smaller constituents, rather than over entire syllables. The syllable-based model operates over indivisible syllable units, while this models treats syllables as combinations of smaller subconstituents.

Once a sequence is syllabified (separating onsets and rhymes), this model uses bigrams over these units to determine word probabilities. Consider again the potential word [lʊkætmi] 'lookatme'. This sequence is first syllabified into onsets and rhymes as [l.ʊ.k.æt.m.i]. Then its phonotactic probability is calculated by multiplying together the bigram probabilities: P(l|#)P(ʊ|l)P(k|ʊ)P(æt|k)P(m|æt)P(i|m)P(#|i). As before, relative frequency estimates are calculated from an (automatically syllabified) unsegmented version of the input corpus.

4 Estimation

Inferring the parameters of these models in an unsupervised way from unsegmented utterances presents a number of challenges. First, a generative model relying on these parameters must be able to accommodate elements and sequences of elements that have not previously been encountered. This includes unseen phonemes, onsets, rhymes, syllables, and unseen sequences of these units. A second difficulty for the generative model arises specifically in the context of segmentation due to the number of boundaries encountered in the input data. In an unsegmented corpus there are no boundaries within an utterance. The only evidence for word boundaries comes from boundaries at the beginnings and ends of utterances. The effect is that the total number of boundaries is lower than the number that must be inferred by the learner, and the overall probability of boundaries is underrepresented in the input data. We considered several estimation methods to overcome these effects.

4.1 Local Minimum Strategy

In previous research (Saffran et al., 1996) it has been suggested that word boundaries are placed at troughs in transitional probability so that a boundary is inserted between two elements when the transitional probability of those elements is lower than the probability of the neighboring transitions. This strategy captures the fact that word boundaries are more likely to occur between elements that have a low probability of occurring together. Since this strategy does not incorporate transitional probabilities into a generative segmentation model, it provides a simple way around the estimation challenges discussed above. We include it for comparison to previous results relying on syllable-based transitional probabilities (Yang, 2004).

4.2 Adjusted Boundary Count Strategy

We also introduce a novel, simple method for adjusting the estimates of transitional probabilities based on input data that underrepresents word boundaries. This method directly adjusts the parameter estimates in order to increase the overall likelihood of word boundaries. The main insight behind this estimation strategy is that observed bigram counts (of co-occurring phonemes, syllables, or onsets and rhymes) in the input data are overestimated since a proportion of them are in reality separated by word boundaries in the desired segmentation. For a given proportion $p_{\#}$ (a parameter of this estimation method), the bigram counts of co-occurring elements (phonemes, syllables, or onsets/rhymes) are systematically decreased by a factor of $(1- p_{\#})$ and for each context c, are reallocated to the transitional probability of $P(\# \mid c)$. The formula below illustrates how this adjustment works for arbitrary contexts c and proportion $p_{\#}$. The probability of each possible element e_i that can follow c is decreased by a factor of $p_{\#}$ as shown in (4). The total probability taken away from all continuations of c is used to increase the probability of $P(\# \mid c)$ as shown in (5).

4) $$P(e_i|c) = \frac{C(ce_i)}{C(c)}(1 - p_{\#})$$

5) $$P(\#|c) = \frac{C(c\#)}{C(c)} + p_{\#}(1 - \frac{C(c\#)}{C(c)})$$

Consider an example for the context x, with three bigrams observed in the input: $c(xy) = 10$, $c(xz) = 6$, and $c(x\#) = 4$. The relative frequency estimates for these transitional probabilities are 0.5, 0.3, and 0.2 respectively. The adjusted count method takes away $p_{\#}$ of the xy and xz counts and reallocates them to $x\#$. For $p_{\#} = 0.5$, for example, the new estimates would be 0.25, 0.15, and 0.6. The adjustment works analogously for every context for each of the units of analysis.

4.3 Smoothing

We also utilized rudimentary smoothing techniques to allow the generative model to deal with unknown sequences. We chose a simple method that allocated non-zero probability to unseen sequences while minimally disrupting the estimates computed using the adjusted boundary count strategy, since our primary concern was in exploring the effects of this novel re-estimation strategy. For all models, add-lambda smoothing (Jurafsky & Martin, 2008) with a value of 0.001 was used. For the syllable-based models this total value was allocated to all unseen bigrams in order to avoid over-allocation of probability to the numerous combinations of unseen syllabic units.

4.4 Iterative Re-estimation

After estimating the transitional probabilities from the unsegmented corpus, the above strategies can be used to compute the optimal segmentation of the input corpus in a single pass. In addition to the above strategies, we also investigated a greedy, iterative re-estimation strategy that makes multiple passes through the corpus. This estimation method takes the output of the above methods and uses it to re-estimate (smoothed and adjusted) parameters for the phonotactic models. It then recomputes the optimal segmentation of the corpus based on the new parameters and repeats until convergence. This method is motivated by previous segmentation work highlighting the effectiveness of greedy re-estimation techniques (Brent, 1999; Venkataraman, 2001; Goldwater et al., 2009; Johnson & Goldwater, 2009). As noted in previous work, such greedy re-estimation has the potential to infer additional word boundaries based on commitments made to word boundaries on earlier passes.

5 Experiments

5.1 Corpus

The experiments for all the models were run on the Brent (1999) version of the Bernstein-Ratner (1987) corpus of English child-directed speech consisting of phonetically transcribed utterances. This corpus has been widely used for evaluating segmentation models. Other models evaluated on this corpus include those of Brent (1999), Venkataraman (2001), Blanchard and Heinz (2008), and Johnson and Goldwater (2009).

5.2 Evaluation

Precision, recall, and f-scores of both word tokens and boundaries were used to evaluate performance. For the models with iterative re-estimation, the reported performance scores are taken from the iteration after convergence. This typically happened after 5-10 iterations.

5.3 Results and Discussion

Table 1 summarizes the word boundary and word token f-scores for all models, while Table 2 presents the precision and recall scores for the best-performing adjusted count models and the local minimum models.

Focusing first on the local minimum estimateion strategy, there are several noteworthy effects. First, our results with local minima for the syllable-level transitional probabilities achieves very similar word token precision and recall to that reported by Yang (2004), who examined a different corpus of child-directed English. The word token precision and recall of our model is 40.2% and 23.7%, respectively, while Yang reported 41.6% and 23.3%, respectively, for his experiments. This corroborates Yang's finding that the local minima estimation strategy for syllable-level transitional probabilities works very poorly, this time showing that this level of performance can be achieved with simultaneous inference of syllabification. As Table 2 shows, the poor performance can be attributed to poor recall, which the low boundary recall and high precision illustrate most clearly. As Yang discusses, the fatal flaw for this approach is that it categorically fails to segment monosyllabic words, which account for an overwhelming majority of words in child-directed speech. This is because local minima must, by definition, be separated by at least one transition with a higher bigram probability, which is not treated as a boundary. Indeed, the proportion of monosyllables is so high that a baseline strategy that simply posits word boundaries at all syllable boundaries achieves a word token f-score of 58.0% using the minimally-supervised syllabification procedure described here[1]. The high performance of the monosyllabic baseline highlights the ineffectiveness of the local minimum strategy but also indicates that syllable structure provides a significant amount of information about word boundaries in English, even if this syllable structure is automatically inferred from unsegmented input using minimal prior knowledge.

Furthermore, our results with the phoneme bigram local minimum strategy (47.1% word token f-score) corroborate Brent's (1999) finding that this method achieves a roughly 50% word token f-score (Brent did not provide exact numbers). The improvement in performance is not surprising given the above discussion about the prevalence of monosyllabic words: local minima defined over the smaller phoneme units do not automatically rule out the possibility of segmenting short words. We also demonstrate that the onset-rhyme model achieves performance similar to that of the syllable bigram model using the local minima strategy. Finally, the results with iterative re-estimation show that further refinement of the posited word boundaries can lead to some improvement, but none of the local minimum models surpass 53% word token f-score, and the syllable-based models perform substantially worse. Overall, these partial results are consistent with the trend suggested by previous work that the syllable-level bigrams examined in the infant studies provide little information about word boundaries in natural language data when the local minimum strategy is used.

However, a different picture emerges when the performance of the adjusted count strategy is considered. The fact that the local minimum strategy is ineffectual is already clear from the comparison with the monosyllabic baseline; however, the results for the adjusted counts estimation strategy reveal that it is possible to ex-

[1] In contrast, Lignos & Yang (2010) report a word token f-score of 78.9% for this baseline for already syllabified input. The difference between these baselines highlights how much more difficult the segmentation task is when the syllabification must be inferred from unsegmented input.

	$p_{\#}=0$		$p_{\#}=0.35$		$p_{\#}=0.5$		$p_{\#}=0.6$		$p_{\#}=0.75$		$p_{\#}=0.99$		LM	
	WF	BF	WF	BF	WF	BF	WF	BF	WF	BF	WF	BF	WF	BF
P	13.0	10.2	34.7	51.9	40.3	60.6	**49.9**	**69.2**	45.9	68.8	13.9	50.1	47.1	64.5
OR	15.4	17.9	28.7	43.3	37.1	55.8	42.2	62.0	**58.4**	**76.0**	52.3	71.4	27.9	44.1
S	10.7	3.1	12.7	8.6	14.2	12.4	15.9	16.3	20.7	26.1	**74.1**	**84.1**	29.8	51.0
P-IR	13.0	10.2	34.7	51.9	40.3	60.6	**50.7**	**69.6**	46.9	69.6	9.9	47.0	52.9	70.5
OR-IR	19.8	29.1	36.8	54.7	47.7	67.7	53.4	72.8	**63.8**	**79.8**	37.1	62.1	42.3	62.3
S-IR	10.9	3.8	13.3	10.5	15.2	15.0	16.8	18.7	23.1	31.4	**79.8**	**88.0**	27.2	43.9

Table 1: Word token (WF) and boundary (BF) f-scores for all models. The columns in the first section of the table represent different settings of the $p_{\#}$ parameter, with highest performance for each adjusted count model shown in bold. $p_{\#}$ values were selected to show a representative range of performance. P = phoneme model; OR = onset-rhyme model; S = syllable model; IR = iterative re-estimation; LM = local minimum strategy. The best performing local minimum model is shaded.

	Adjusted Count Estimation				Local Minimum Estimation			
	WP	WR	BP	BR	WP	WR	BP	BR
P-IR	50.3	51.1	68.8	70.4	53.4	52.4	71.5	69.5
OR-IR	63.8	63.8	79.9	79.8	44.2	40.5	66.5	58.6
S-IR	85.2	75.0	97.0	80.6	40.4	20.5	94.0	28.6

Table 2: Word precision (WP), word recall (WR), boundary precision (BP), and boundary recall (BR) scores for selected models. For the adjusted count estimation models, the results for the best performing parameter value are shown (P-IR: 0.6; OR-IR: 0.75; S-IR: 0.99).

extract substantially more information about word boundaries from syllable-based models when these cues are used in the context of a generative model and better methods are used for unsupervised estimation of these parameters. In fact, using the adjusted counts estimation method with the optimal parameter settings, the reverse trend is observed, wherein the phoneme-level bigrams perform worse than the syllable-based models, and syllable-level bigrams perform best of all, reaching word token f-scores of nearly 80%. Crucially, both the onset-rhyme and the syllable bigram models achieve levels of performance that surpass the monosyllabic baseline. In the case of the syllable bigram, the improvement in word token f-score is more than 20% when iterative re-estimation is used and more than 15% when segmentation is performed in only a single pass through the corpus.

The phoneme-based models perform about as well whether adjusted counts or local minimum estimation is used. However, compensation for the underrepresentation of word boundaries in the input is crucial to the syllable-based models. These models surpass the local minimum estimation models only when the $p_{\#}$ parameter compensates sufficiently for the input bias against word boundaries. As shown in Table 1, without any compensation ($p_{\#}=0$), all models perform terribly. This is because utterance boundaries provide very little evidence of word boundaries, and the models estimated directly from such input massively undersegment. It is only at higher settings of the parameter that performance improves. As expected, the optimal parameter value increases with the granularity of the unit over which bigrams are computed. This makes sense since boundaries are more likely to fall between larger units than between smaller units.

Less expected is the fact that the optimal parameter values are high compared to the empirical rates of word boundaries in the true segmentation of the input corpus. For example, the true rate of utterance-internal word boundaries is around 30% at the phoneme level, yet the optimal $p_{\#}$ value for phoneme bigrams is around 60%. The reason for this is that our generative model, like that of a number of previous models discussed in the literature (Brent, 1999; Venkataraman, 2001; Goldwater et al., 2009), has an inherent undersegmentation bias. Due to the way the phonotactic models are defined, there is a cost for every additional word boundary posited in the segmentation. This is because positing a boundary corresponds to the generation of an additional symbol, #, which otherwise does not have to be generated. Since generating a # is never done with 100% probability, doing so always incurs a cost relative to a segmentation where no such # has to be generated. The high optimal settings of the $p_{\#}$ parameter reflect this inherent bias and enable the estimation procedure to compensate not only for the underrepresentation of word boundaries in the input but also for this bias in the generative model.

6 Conclusions

We compared segmentation models that rely on phoneme transitions to models that make use of syllable structure. The results indicate that syllable-based statistics are valuable for segmentation. We also showed that it is possible to utilize this structure successfully with limited prior knowledge of the target language by using a simple syllabification strategy inferred from unsegmented utterances. The performance of the syllable-based models also demonstrates that it is possible to achieve good segmentation results without the use of a lexicon. Another contribution of this work is a novel estimation procedure that addresses some challenges of unsupervised segmentation. We showed that adjusting parameter estimates inferred from unsegmented input is essential for achieving good performance.

The strong performance of the syllable level bigram phonotactic model has a number of implications. First, it demonstrates that the kind of statistical regularities that infants have been consistently shown to be sensitive to in artificial experimental stimuli do provide a substantial amount of information about word boundaries in natural language data, at least in English. This lends significant credibility to the claim that sensitivity to such statistical regularities plays a crucial role in infants' early language development (contra Yang 2004). This result also highlights the role that sensitivity to richer phonological information, beyond the level of phonemes, plays in language learning, a result that is echoed in much recent work on the modeling of phonotactic well-formedness of isolated words (Hayes & Wilson, 2008; Albright, 2009; Daland et al., 2011). A consistent finding of this work has been that access to abstract structure and robust generalization mechanisms is crucial to the modeling of human phonotactic knowledge. While our results are compatible with these conclusions, our results cannot confirm that it is syllable structure *per se* that improves segmentation since the syllable-based models have several co-occurring advantages. In addition to abstract structure, they can track longer and more complex dependencies. Nonetheless, these results motivate further investigation into the role that richer models of phonotactics may play in word segmentation and into the precise mechanisms responsible for improved segmentation using syllable structure. Particularly critical is exploration of phonotactically-based segmentation models for languages besides English, for which phonotactic cues hold significant promise (Jarosz & Johnson, 2013) given the relatively low performance of state-of-the-art lexicon-building models (Johnson 2008b).

Another important direction for future work is investigating how early, phonotactically-based segmentation interacts with subsequent learning of higher-level structure, including the lexicon. Johnson (2008a) and Johnson & Goldwater (2009) have already demonstrated that syllable structure provides valuable information in this context; however, their models relied on very different syllable regularities than those investigated here, and the consequences of these differences should be explored in future work.

Goldwater et al. (2009) showed that a number of proposed segmentation models have an undersegmentation bias that can be avoided by simultaneously modeling statistical dependencies between words. They proposed a Bayesian prior to favor a smaller lexicon and showed that otherwise unigram models introduce a severe undersegmentation bias due to the possibility of matching empirical probabilities by memorizing utterances as words. Note that the same is not true of syllable-based models since the hypothesis space does not permit memorization of utterances, and the size of the syllable inventory, unlike a lexicon, remains relatively stable under different segmentations. Thus, the syllable-based models are not subject to the same kind of undersegmentation bias. Interestingly, the syllable bigram model surpasses the performance of the word bigram model proposed by Goldwater et al. (word token f-score 72.3) given sufficient compensation for its undersegmentation bias. However, this level of performance requires adjustment of the $p_{\#}$ parameter to compensate for the cost of generating additional boundaries. Although parameters are common in computational models (for example, Goldwater et al. used a $p_{\#}$ parameter to modulate the prior distributions in their Bayesian models), they do not provide a particularly satisfying explanation for why infants are compelled to break up the speech stream into smaller units (words). Further work is needed to determine how undersegmentation biases are ultimately overcome by children.

References

Adriaans, Frans and Kager, René. 2010. Adding generalization to statistical learning: The induction of phonotactics from continuous speech. *Journal of Memory and Language* 62(3): 311-331.

Albright, Adam. 2009. Feature-based generalisation as a source of gradient acceptability. *Phonology*, 26(1): 9-41.

Aslin, Richard N., Saffran, Jenny R., & Newport, Elissa L. 1998. Computation of conditional probability statistics by 8-month-old infants. *Psychological Science*, 9, 321-324.

Bernstein-Ratner, Nan. 1987. The phonology of parent child speech. *Children's Language*, 6: 159-174.

Blanchard, Daniel and Heinz, Jeffrey. 2008. Improving word segmentation by simultaneously learning phonotactics. In *Conll '08: Proceedings of the 12th Conference on Computational Natural Language Learning.* Stroudsburg, PA: Association for Computational Linguistics.

Blanchard, Daniel, Heinz, Jeffrey and Golinkoff, Roberta. 2010. Modeling the contribution of phonotactic cues to the problem of word segmentation. *Journal of Child Language,* 37(3): 487-511.

Brent, Michael R. 1999. An efficient, probabilistically sound algorithm for segmentation and word discovery. *Machine Learning*, 34(1-3): 71-105.

Daland, Robert and Pierrehumbert, Janet B. 2011. Learning Diphone-Based Segmentation. *Cognitive science,* 35(1). Wiley Online Library. 119–155.

Daland, Robert, Hayes, Bruce, White, James, Garellek, Marc, Davis, Andrea and Norrmann, Ingrid. 2011. Explaining sonority projection effects. *Phonology*, 28(2): 197-234.

Dale, P. S., & Fenson, L. 1996. Lexical development norms for young children. *Behavior Research Methods, Instruments, & Computers*, 28, 125-127.

Goldwater, Sharon, Griffiths, Thomas L. and Johnson, Mark. 2009. A Bayesian framework for word segmentation: Exploring the effects of context. *Cognition*, 112(1): 21-54.

Hayes, Bruce & Wilson, Colin. 2008. A maximum entropy model of phonotactics and phonotactic learning. *Linguistic Inquiry*, 39(3): 379-440.

Hockema, Stephen A. 2006. Finding Words in Speech: An Investigation of American English. *Language Learning and Development,* 2(2). Psychology Press. 119-146.

Jarosz, Gaja and Johnson, J. Alex. 2013. The Richness of Distributional Cues to Word Boundaries in Speech to Young Children. *Language Learning and Development*, 9(2): 175-210.

Johnson, Mark. 2008a. Using adaptor grammars to identify synergies in the unsupervised acquisition of linguistic structure. *Proceedings of the 46th Annual Meeting of the Association for Computational Linguistics*. Association for Computational Linguistics.

Johnson, Mark. 2008b. Unsupervised Word Segmentation for Sesotho Using Adaptor Grammars. *Proceedings of the 10th Meeting of ACL SIGMORPHON.* Columbus, OH: Association of Computational Linguistics.

Johnson, Mark & Goldwater, Sharon. 2009. Improving nonparametric Bayesian inference: Experiments on unsupervised word segmentation with adaptor grammars. In *NAACL '09: Proceedings of the Annual Conference of the North American Chapter of the Association for Computational Linguistics.* Boulder, CO: Association for Computational Linguistics.

Jurafsky, Daniel & Martin, James H. 2008. Speech and language processing, 2nd edition. Upper Saddle River, NJ: Prentice-Hall.

Jusczyk, Peter W. & Luce, Paul A. 1994. Infants' Sensitivity to Phonotactic Patterns in the Native Language. *Journal of Memory and Language*, 33(5): 630-645.

Lignos, Constantine and Yang, Charles. 2010. Recession Segmentation: Simpler Online Word Segmentation Using Limited Resources. *Proceedings of the Fourteenth Conference on Computational Natural Language Learning.* (CoNLL '10). Association for Computational Linguistics. .

Mattys, Sven L. and Jusczyk, Peter W. 2000. Phonotactic cues for segmentation of fluent speech by infants. *Cognition*, 78(2): 91-121.

Mattys, Sven L., Jusczyk, Peter W., Luce, Paul A., and Morgan, James L. 1999. Phonotactic and prosodic effects on word segmentation in infants. *Cognitive psychology*, 38(4): 465-494.

Newport, Elissa L. and Aslin, Richard N. 2004. Learning at a distance I. Statistical learning of non-adjacent dependencies. *Cognitive psychology*, 48(2): 127-162.

Pelucchi, Bruna, Hay, Jessica F., and Saffran, Jenny R. 2009. Learning in reverse: Eight-month-old infants track backward transitional probabilities. *Cognition*, 113(2): 244-247.

Saffran, Jenny R., Aslin, Richard N., and Newport, Elissa L. 1996. Statistical learning by 8-month-old infants. *Science*, 274(5294): 1926-1928.

Swingley, Daniel. 2005. Statistical clustering and the contents of the infant vocabulary. *Cognitive Psychology*, 50(1): 86-32.

Thiessen, Erik D. and Saffran, Jenny R. 2003. When cues collide: use of stress and statistical cues to word boundaries by 7-to 9-month-old infants. *Developmental psychology,* 39(4): 706.

Venkataraman, Anand 2001. A statistical model for word discovery in transcribed speech. *Computational Linguistics*, 27(3): 352-372.

Yang, Charles D. 2004. Universal Grammar, statistics or both? *Trends in Cognitive Sciences*, 8(10): 451-456.

Generalizing inflection tables into paradigms with finite state operations

Mans Hulden
University of Helsinki
mans.hulden@helsinki.fi

Abstract

Extracting and performing an alignment of the longest common subsequence in inflection tables has been shown to be a fruitful approach to supervised learning of morphological paradigms. However, finding the longest subsequence common to multiple strings is well known to be an intractable problem. Additional constraints on the solution sought complicate the problem further—such as requiring that the particular subsequence extracted, if there is ambiguity, be one that is best alignable in an inflection table. In this paper we present and discuss the design of a tool that performs the extraction through some advanced techniques in finite state calculus and does so efficiently enough for the practical purposes of inflection table generalization.

1 Introduction

Supervised learning of morphological paradigms from inflection tables has recently been approached from a number of directions. One approach is given in Hulden et al. (2014), where morphological paradigm induction is performed by extracting the longest common subsequence (LCS) from a set of words representing an inflection table. Although that work presents encouraging results as regards learning morphological paradigms from inflection tables, no details are given as to how the paradigms themselves are extracted. The purpose of this paper is to describe how such a paradigm extraction procedure can be performed using only finite state operations.

Extracting the longest common subsequence from a large number of strings is known as the multiple longest common subsequence problem (MLCS), and is computationally intractable. In fields like bioinformatics specialized heuristic algorithms have been developed for efficiently extracting common subsequences from DNA sequences. In linguistics applications where the goal is to extract common patterns in an inflection table, however, the problem manifests itself in a different guise. While most applications in other fields work with a small number of fairly long sequences, inflection tables may contain hundreds of short sequences. Additionally, it is not enough to extract the LCS from an inflection table. The LCS itself is often ambiguous and may be factorized in several different ways in a table. This means that we operate under the additional constraint that the LCS must not only be found, but, in case of ambiguity, its most contiguous factorization must also be indicated, as this often produces linguistically interesting generalizations.

In this paper we will address the problem of extracting the minimal MLCS through entirely finite state means. Finite state methods lend themselves to solving this kind of an optimization problem concisely, and, as it turns out, also efficiently enough for practical purposes.

This paper is laid out as follows. First, we outline the MLCS-based approach to supervised learning of morphological paradigms in section 2. We then describe in broad strokes the algorithm required for generalizing inflection tables into paradigms in section 3. Next, we give a finite state implementation of the algorithm in section 4, followed by a brief discussion of a stand-alone software tool based on this that extracts paradigms from collections of inflection tables in section 5.

2 Supervised learning of morphological paradigms

In the following, we operate with the central idea of a model of word formation that organizes word forms and their inflection patterns into paradigms (Hockett, 1954; Robins, 1959; Matthews, 1972;

Proceedings of the 2014 Joint Meeting of SIGMORPHON and SIGFSM, pages 29–36,
Baltimore, Maryland USA, June 27 2014. ©2014 Association for Computational Linguistics

Stump, 2001). In particular, we model paradigms in a slightly more abstract manner than is customarily done. For the purposes of this paper, we differentiate between a paradigm and an inflection table in the following way: an inflection table is simply a list of words that represents a concrete manifestation, or instantiation, of a paradigm. A paradigm is also a list of words, but with special symbols that represent variables interspersed. These variables, when instantiated, represent particular strings shared across an inflection table.

In our representation, this kind of an *abstract paradigm* is an ordered collection of strings, where each string may additionally contain interspersed variables denoted $x_1, x_2, \ldots, x_n$. The strings represent fixed, obligatory parts of a paradigm, while the variables represent mutable parts. A complete *abstract paradigm* captures some generalization where the mutable parts represented by variables are instantiated the same way for all forms in one particular inflection table. For example, the fairly simple paradigm

$$x_1 \quad x_1\textbf{+s} \quad x_1\textbf{+ed} \quad x_1\textbf{+ing}$$

could represent a set of English verb forms, where x_1 in this case would coincide with the infinitive form of the verb—**walk**, **climb**, **look**, etc.[1]

2.1 Learning paradigms from inflection tables

As is seen from the above example, a general enough paradigm can encode the inflection pattern of a large number of words. When learning such paradigms from data—i.e. complete inflection tables—we intuitively want to find the 'common' elements of a table and generalize those.

The core of the method is to factor the word forms in an inflection table in such a manner that the elements common to all entries are declared variables, while the non-common elements are assumed to be part of the inflection pattern. To illustrate the idea with an example, consider a shortened inflection table for the regular German verb **holen** (to fetch):[2]

hole#holst#holt#holen#holt#holen#geholt (1)

Obviously, in this example, the element common to each entry in the inflection table is **hol**. Declaring **hol** to be a variable, we can rewrite the inflection table as:

$$x_1\textbf{+e\#}x_1\textbf{+st\#}x_1\textbf{+t\#}x_1\textbf{+en\#}x_1\textbf{+t\#}x_1\textbf{+en\#ge+}x_1\textbf{+t} \quad (2)$$

This extraction of the 'common elements' is formalized in Hulden et al. (2014) to be equivalent to extraction of the *longest common subsequence* of the strings $w_1, \ldots, w_n$ in an inflection table.[3] The purpose of extracting the common parts and labeling them variables is to provide a model for generalization of inflection patterns. Under the assumption that a variable x_i in this paradigm representation corresponds to a nonempty string, we can instantiate an inflection table by simply providing the variable strings $x_1, \ldots, x_n$. Thus, we can talk about a paradigm-generating function

$$f : (x_1, \ldots, x_n) \to \Sigma^*$$

that maps instantiations of variables to a string representing the complete inflection table, in this case a string where entries are #-separated.

To illustrate this, consider the simple paradigm in (2). It implicitly defines a function f where, for example, f(**kauf**) maps to the string

kaufe#kaufst#kauft#kaufen#kauft#kaufen#gekauft (3)

i.e. produces the inflection table for the regular verb **kaufen** (to buy), which behaves like **holen**. Likewise, we can also consider the inverse function. Given an unknown word form, e.g. **macht** (to make, 3pSg), we can see that the only way it fits the paradigm in (2) is if it comes from an inflection table:

mache#machst#macht#machen#macht#machen#gemacht (4)

that is, if **macht** is part of the output for f(**mach**).

[1] Our formalization of a paradigm of strings and intervening variables bears many similarities to so-called *pattern languages* (Angluin, 1980). In fact, each entry in a paradigm could be considered a separate pattern language. Additionally, all the individual pattern languages in one paradigm are constrained to share the same variables and the variables are constrained to collectively be instantiated the same way.

[2] We follow the convention that entries in an inflection table are separated by #.

[3] Not to be confused with the longest common *substring*, which is a different problem, solvable in polynomial time for n strings. Subsequences may be discontinuous while substrings may not. For example, assume $s = abcaa$ and $t = dbcadaa$. The longest common substring shared by the two is bca obtained from s by $a\underline{bca}a$ and t by $d\underline{bca}daa$. By contrast, the longest common subsequence is $bcaa$, obtained from s by $a\underline{bcaa}$ and t by $d\underline{bca}d\underline{a}a$ or $d\underline{bca}da\underline{a}$ or $d\underline{b}c\underline{a}d\underline{aa}$.

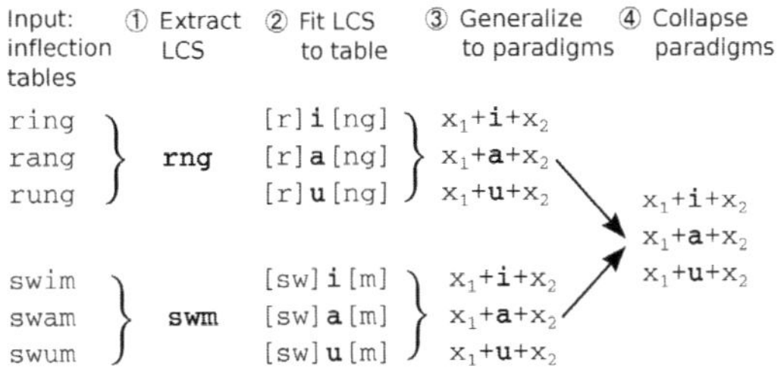

Figure 1: Paradigm extraction strategy.

In other words, the extraction of multiple common longest subsequences (MLCS) from inflection tables immediately provides a (simple) generalization mechanism of a grammar, and also suggests a supervised learning strategy for morphological paradigms. In conjunction with statistical machine learning methods, Hulden et al. (2014) has shown that the paradigm extraction and generalization method provides competitive results in various supervised and semi-supervised NLP learning tasks. One such task is to provide a hypothetical reconstruction of a complete inflection table from an unseen base form after first witnessing a number of complete inflection tables. Another task is the semi-supervised collection of lexical entries and matching them to paradigms by observing distributions of word forms across all the possible paradigms they can fit into. In general, there is much current interest in similar tasks in NLP; see e.g. Dreyer and Eisner (2011); Durrett and DeNero (2013); Eskander et al. (2013) for a variety of current methods.

3 Learning method

The basic procedure as outlined by Hulden et al. (2014) for learning paradigms from inflection tables can be represented by the four-step procedure given in figure 1. Here, multiple inflection tables are gathered, and the LCS to each table is found individually. Following that, the LCS is fit into the table, and contiguous segments that participate in the LCS are labeled variables. After paradigm generalization, it may turn out that several identical paradigms have been learned, which may then be collapsed.

The first two steps of the method dictate that one:

1. Extract the longest common subsequence (LCS) to all the entries in the inflection table.
2. Split the LCS(s)—of which there may be several—into variables in such a way that the number of variables is minimized. Two segments xy are always part of the same variable if they occur together in every form of an inflection table. If some substring z intervenes between x and y in some form, x and y must be assigned separate variables.

These steps represent steps ① and ② in figure 1. After the variables have been identified, steps ③ and ④ in the figure are easily accomplished by non-finite-state means.

In the following, we will focus on the previously unaddressed problem of finding the LCS of an inflection table (①), and of distributing possible variables corresponding to contiguous sequences of the LCS in a way that gives rise to the minimum number of variables (②).

4 Finite-state implementation

The main challenge in producing a paradigm from an inflection table is not the extraction of the longest common subsequences, but rather, doing so with the added criterion of minimizing the number of variables used. Extracting the LCS from multiple strings is known to be NP-hard (Maier, 1978) and naive implementations will fail quickly for even a moderate number of strings found in inflection tables. While there exist specialized algorithms that attempt to efficiently either calculate (Irving and Fraser, 1992) or approximate (Wang et al., 2010) the LCS, we find that extraction can easily be accomplished with a simple transducer calculation. The task of ascertaining that the LCS is distributed in such a way as to minimize the number of variables turns out to be more challenging; at the same time, however, it is a problem to which the finite state calculus is particularly well suited, as will be seen below.

4.1 Notation and tool

The paradigm extraction tool was implemented with the help of the *foma* toolkit (Hulden, 2009). In the actual implementation, instead of directly compiling regular expressions, we make use of *foma*'s programming API, but in the following we give regular expression equivalents to the method used. Table 1 contains a summary of the regular expression notation used.

`0`	Empty string
`?`	Any symbol in alphabet
`.#.`	End or beginning of string
`{xyz}`	String
`AB`	Concatenation
`A*, A+`	Kleene star, Kleene plus
`A|B`	Union
`A & B`	Intersection
`A - B`	Difference
`~A`	Complement
`A .o. B`	Composition
`%`	Escape symbol
`[` and `]`	Grouping brackets
`A:B`	Cross product
`T.2`	Output projection of T
`A -> B`	Rewrite A as B
`_eq(X,L,R)`	Strings between L,R are equal
`def W {word}`	Define FSM constant
`def F(X,Y) X Y`	Regular expression macro

Table 1: Regular expression notation in *foma*.

4.2 LCS extraction

As the first step, we assume that we have encoded each word $w_1, \ldots, w_n$ in an inflection table as an automaton that accepts that word.[4]

In general, we can define the set of subsequences of any word by a general regular expression technique:

```
def SS(X) [X .o. [?|?:0]*].2;
```

`SS(`w`)` then contains all of the subsequences of some word w. Taking advantage of this, we may calculate the intersection of each set of subsequences `SS(`w_1`) & ...& SS(`w_n`)`, producing the language that contains all the common subsequences to $w_1, \ldots, w_n$. From this, extracting the longest subsequence or sequences could in principle be performed by inspecting the resulting automaton, but the same can also be done algebraically for finite sets:

```
def Max(X) X -
  [[X .o. [?:a]* [?:0]+].2 .o. [a:?]*].2;
```

Here, `Max(X)` is a regular expression technique of extracting the set of longest strings from an automaton. We achieve this in practice by first changing all symbols in `X` to an arbitrary symbol (`a` in this case), removing at least one symbol from the end, and using this intermediate result to remove from `X` all strings shorter than the maximum.[5]

An automaton that contains all LCSs for a set of words $w_1, \ldots, w_n$ can thus be calculated as:

`Max(SS(`w_1`) & ... & SS(`w_n`))` (5)

The above two lines together represent a surprisingly efficient manner of calculating the MLCS for a large number of relatively similar short sequences (less than 100 characters) and is essentially equivalent to performing the same calculation through dynamic programming algorithms with some additional search heuristics.

4.3 Minimizing variables

We can then assume that we have calculated the LCS or LCSs for an inflection table and can represent it as an automaton. The following step is to assign variables to segments that can correspond to the LCS in a minimal way. The minimality requirement is crucial for good generalization as is seen in the illustration here:

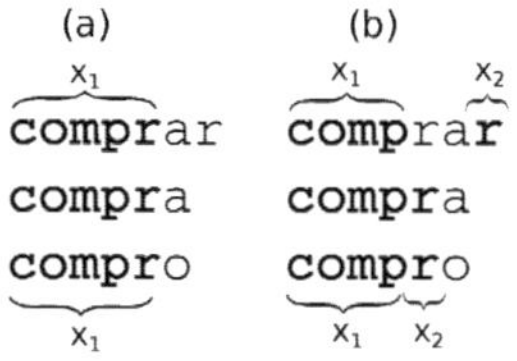

The above shows two ways of breaking up the LCS **compr** in the hypothetical three-word inflection table for Spanish. In case (a) the **compr** has been located contiguously in inflection entries, while in (b) there is a gap in the first form, leading to the inevitable use of two variables to generalize the table.

In the finite-state string encoding, the overall intent of our effort to calculate the minimum-variable MLCS assignment in the table is to produce an automaton that contains the divisions of variables marked up with brackets. For example, given a hypothetical two-word table **holen#geholt**, the LCS is obviously **hol**. Now, there are several valid divisions of **hol** into variables, e.g. **[ho][l]en#ge[ho][l]t**, which would represent a two-variable division, while

[4]We abuse notation slightly by representing by w_i both a word and an automaton that accepts that word.

[5]This is a rather inefficient way of extracting the set of longest strings from an automaton. However, as the runtime of this part represents only a minute fraction of the complete procedure, we do so to preserve the benefit of clarity that using finite-state calculus offers.

pextract example

```
1  def SS(X) [X .o. [?|?:0]*].2;
2  def Max(X) X - [[X .o. ?:a* ?:0+].2 .o. a:?*].2;
3  def RedupN(X,Y) [_eq([LEFT X RIGHT [Y LEFT X RIGHT]*], LEFT, RIGHT) .o. LEFT|RIGHT -> 0].l;
4  def NOBR ? - %[ - %] - %#;
5  def Order(X) [[X .o. 0:%# ?* 0:%#                            .o.
6                  ?* %# [NOBR | %[:%< | %]:%>]* %# ?*          .o.
7                  %[|%] -> 0                                   .o.
8                  [?* 0:%> 0:%< \[%<|%>|%[|%] ]+ %> ?*]*       .o.
9                  %#:0 ?* %#:0                                 .o.
10                 0 -> %[|%] .o. %< -> %[ .o. %> -> %]] .o. X ].2;
11 def MarkRoot(X) [X .o. [?|0:%[ ?+ 0:%]]* ].2;
12 def RandomBracketing(X) [X .o. [? | 0:%[ NOBR* 0:%]]* ].2;
13 def AddExtraSegments(X) [X .o. [0:NOBR* | %[ \%]* %] | %#]* ].2;
14 def Filter(X) X - Order(X);
15
16 def Table              {hole#holst#holt#holen#holt#holen#geholt};
17 def MLCS Max(SS({hole}) & SS({holst}) & SS({holt}) & SS({holen}) & SS({holt}) & SS({holen}) & SS({geholt}));
18 def BracketedMLCS      AddExtraSegments(RedupN(MarkRoot(MLCS), %#));
19 def BracketedTable     RandomBracketing(Table);
20
21 regex Filter(BracketedMLCS & BracketedTable);
22 print words
```

Figure 2: Complete implementation of the extraction of the minimum-variable longest common subsequences as a *foma*-script. Here, a small German verb table is hard-coded for illustration purposes on lines 16 and 17. The output is **[hol]e#[hol]st#[hol]t#[hol]en#[hol]t#[hol]en#ge[hol]t**

[hol]en#ge[hol]t would represent a one-variable division.

Naturally, these brackets will have to be divided in such a way that there is no better way to achieve the division—i.e. no markup such that fewer variables are instantiated.

The crux of the method used here is to first produce an automaton that accepts the set of *all* valid markups of the MLCS in the table string, and then use that set to in turn define the set of suboptimal markups. Similar finite-state techniques have been used by Gerdemann and van Noord (2000); Eisner (2002); Karttunen (2010); Gerdemann and Hulden (2012), to, among other things, define suboptimal candidates in Optimality Theory. The trick is to set up a transducer T that contains the input-output pair (x, x'), iff x' represents a worse division of variables than x does. In effect, T captures the transitive closure of an ordering relation $\succ$ of the various factorizations of the strings into variables, and T contains the string pair (x, x') when $x \succ^{+} x'$. In general, supposing that we have an identity transducer, i.e. automaton A, and a transducer T that maps strings in A according to the transitive closure of an ordering relation $\succ$, then we can always remove the suboptimal strings according to $\succ$ from A by calculating $A - \text{range}(A \circ T)$.

Apart from this central idea, some bookkeeping is required because we are working with string representations of inflection tables. A complete *foma* listing that captures the behavior of our implementation is given in figure 2. The main complication in the program is to produce the transitive closure of the ordering by setting up a transducer `Order` that, given some bracketed string, breaks up continuous sequences of brackets into discontinuities, e.g. **[xyz]** $\rightarrow$ **[x][yz]**,**[xy][z]**, **[x][y][z]**.

The main logic of the program appears on lines 18–21. The `BracketedMLCS` is the language where the MLCS has been bracketed in various ways and extra segments inserted arbitrarily. An extra complication is that the MLCS must always be bracketed the same way within a string, e.g. **[xy][z]#...#[xy][z]**, or **[x][yz]#...#[x][yz]** etc. That is, the variable splits have to be equal across entries.

The `BracketedTable` language is the language that contains a string that represents the inflection table at hand, but with arbitrary bracketings. The intersection of the two languages then contain the valid MLCS bracketings of the inflection table. After the intersection is calculated, we apply the ordering transducer and filter out those strings with suboptimal bracket markup. Figure 3 illustrates the process.

4.4 Optimizations and additions

In addition to the description given above, the actual implementation contains a number of secondary optimization strategies. The foremost one is the simple preprocessing move to locate first the longest common prefix p in the inflection table before any processing is done. This can, of course, be discovered very efficiently. The prefix

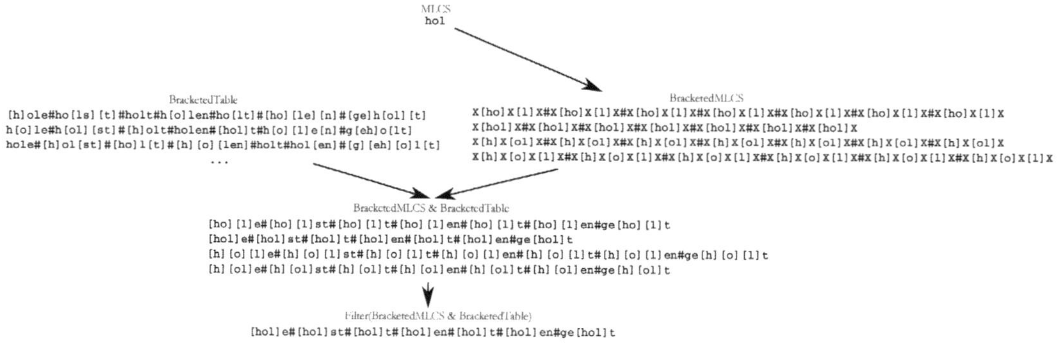

Figure 3: Illustrated steps in the process of extracting and identifying the MLCS. The `MLCS` language contains only the longest common subsequence(s). From that language, the language `BracketedMLCS` is generated, which contains arbitrary strings with the MLCS bracketed in different ways (`X` here represents any string from Σ^*). Intersecting that language with the `BracketedTable` language and filtering out suboptimal bracketings yields the final generalization.

can be set aside until the main algorithm is completed, and then attached as a separate variable to the paradigm that was extracted without p. This has little noticeable effect in most cases, but does speed up the variable minimization with large tables that contains words more than 30 characters long. Although not included in the implementation, the same maneuver can subsequently be performed on the longest common suffix of the remaining string after the prefix is extracted.

Additionally, there are still residual cases where the LCS may be located in several ways with the same number of variables. An actual example comes from a Swedish paradigm with two options: **[sege]l#[seg]l[e]n#[seg]l[e]t** vs. **[seg]e[l]#[segl]en#[segl]et**. The ambiguity here is due to the two equally long LCSs **sege** and **segl**. These are resolved in our implementation through non-finite-state means by choosing the division that results in the smallest number of infix-segments.

5 Implementation

We have implemented the above paradigm extractor as a freely available stand-alone tool `pextract`.[6] The utility reads inflection tables, generalizes them into paradigms and collapses resulting identical paradigms. Steps ③ and ④ in figure 1 are trivially performed by non-finite state means. After paradigm generalization, bracketed sequences are replaced by variable symbols (step ③). As each paradigm is then represented as a single string, paradigm collapsing can be performed by simply testing string equivalence.

The tool also implements some further global restrictions on the nature of the generalizations allowed. These include, for example, a linguistically motivated attempt to minimize the number of infixes in paradigms. It also stores information (see figure 4) about the components of generalizations: the variable instantiations seen, etc., which may be useful for subsequent tools that take advantage of its output.[7]

Figure 4 briefly illustrates through a toy example the input and output to the extraction tool: inputs are simply lists of entries in inflection tables, with or without morphological information, and the output is a list of paradigms where numbers correspond to variables. In the event that several paradigms can be collapsed, the tool collapses them (as indeed is seen in figure 4). The actual instantiations of the variables seen are also stored, represented by the digits 1, . . . as are the complete first (often base) forms, represented by 0. In effect, all the seen inflection tables can in principle be reconstructed from the resulting abstract paradigms.

Table 2 shows how the `pextract` tool generalizes with five data sets covering German (DE), Spanish (ES), and Finnish (FI), provided by Durrett and DeNero (2013), along with running times. Here, among other things, we see that the tool has generalized 3,855 Spanish verb inflection ta-

[6] `http://pextract.googlecode.com`

[7] Statistical information about what the variables looked like during generalization can be useful information when performing classifying tasks, such as attempting to fit previously unseen words to already learned paradigms, etc.

```
katabtu   perf-1-sg                      1+a+2+a+3+tu#1+a+2+a+3+ta#1+u+2+i+3+u#1+u+2+i+3+na
katabta   perf-2-m-sg                    0=katabtu
kutibu    pass-perf-3-m-pl               1=k
kutibna   pass-perf-3-f-pl               2=t
                            pextract
                            ------>      3=b
darastu   perf-1-sg                      0=darastu
darasta   perf-2-m-sg                    1=d
durisu    pass-perf-3-m-pl               2=r
durisna   pass-perf-3-f-pl               3=s
```

Figure 4: Paradigm extraction tool. For the two toy Arabic inflection tables on the left, the `pextract` tool produces one three-variable paradigm as output, and reports how the three variables have been instantiated in the example data, and also how the first form (presumably often the base form) appeared in its entirety.

bles into 97 distinct paradigms, and 6,200 Finnish nouns and adjectives have been reduced to 258 paradigms. For comparison, the fairly complete Thompson (1998) lists 79 classes of Spanish verbs, while the Kotus (2007) grammar description counts 51 Finnish noun and adjective paradigms.

Much of the remaining redundancy in resulting paradigms can be attributed to lack of phonological modeling. That is, paradigms could be further collapsed if phonological alternations were added subsequently to paradigm extraction. Consider a selection of four forms from the inflection table for the Finnish verb **aidata** (to fence):

aidata#aitaan#aitaat#aitasin (6)

This is generalized by the tool into

$$x_1\mathbf{+d+}x_2\mathbf{+ta\#}x_1\mathbf{+t+}x_2\mathbf{+an\#}x_1\mathbf{+t+}x_2\mathbf{+at\#}x_1\mathbf{+t+}x_2\mathbf{+sin} \quad (7)$$

The generalization is indeed correct, but the method does not take into account a general phonological process of consonant gradation where **t** and **d** alternate depending on the syllable type. With this additional information, paradigm tables could in principle be collapsed further and this particular paradigm merged with a more general paradigm learned for Finnish verbs. The same goes for other phonological processes which sometimes cause the tool to produce superficially different paradigms that could be collapsed further by modeling vowel harmony and other phenomena.

We may note that the word lengths and inflection table sizes encountered in the wild are far larger than the examples used in this article. For the Wiktionary data, for example, many inflection tables have more than 50 entries and word lengths of 50 characters.

Data	**Input: inflection tables**	**Output: abstract paradigms**	**Comp. time(s)**
DE-VERBS	1,827	140	123.6
DE-NOUNS	2,564	70	73.5
ES-VERBS	3,855	97	144.9
FI-VERBS	7,049	282	432.2
FI-NOUNS-ADJS	6,200	258	374.1

Table 2: Paradigm generalization from Wiktionary-gathered inflection tables.

6 Conclusion

In this work, we have presented a method for extracting general paradigms from inflection tables through entirely finite state means. This involves solving a constrained longest common subsequence problem, for which the calculus offered by modern finite state toolkits is well suited. Although the problem in no way requires a finite state solution, we find that addressing it with a general-purpose programming language appears far more complex a route.

We further note that finite state transducers can be profitably employed after paradigm generalization has occurred—to find all possible paradigms and slots that an unknown word form might fit into, to generate paradigms from base forms, and so forth.

An interesting further potential optimization is to try to address ambiguous LCS assignments with the completely different strategy of attempting to maximize similarity across paradigms, or minimize the number of resulting paradigms, assuming one is generalizing a batch of inflection tables at the same time. Additionally, modeling phonological phenomena as a separate step after morphological paradigm generalization provides opportunities for further development of the system.

Acknowledgements

This article was much improved by the insightful comments provided by the anonymous reviewers. The research was partially funded by the Academy of Finland under grant agreement 258373, *Machine learning of rules in natural language morphology and phonology*. Additional important support was provided by the Centre for Language Technology and Språkbanken at the University of Gothenburg, where part of this research was undertaken.

References

Angluin, D. (1980). Finding patterns common to a set of strings. *Journal of Computer and System Sciences*, 21(1):46–62.

Dreyer, M. and Eisner, J. (2011). Discovering morphological paradigms from plain text using a Dirichlet process mixture model. In *Proceedings of the Conference on Empirical Methods in Natural Language Processing*, pages 616–627. Association for Computational Linguistics.

Durrett, G. and DeNero, J. (2013). Supervised learning of complete morphological paradigms. In *Proceedings of NAACL-HLT*, pages 1185–1195.

Eisner, J. (2002). Comprehension and compilation in optimality theory. In *Proceedings of the 40th Annual Meeting on Association for Computational Linguistics*, pages 56–63. Association for Computational Linguistics.

Eskander, R., Habash, N., and Rambow, O. (2013). Automatic extraction of morphological lexicons from morphologically annotated corpora. In *Proceedings of the 2013 Conference on Empirical Methods in Natural Language Processing*, pages 1032–1043. Association for Computational Linguistics.

Gerdemann, D. and Hulden, M. (2012). Practical finite state optimality theory. In *10th International Workshop on Finite State Methods and Natural Language Processing*, page 10.

Gerdemann, D. and van Noord, G. (2000). Approximation and exactness in finite state optimality theory. In *Proceedings of the Fifth Workshop of the ACL Special Interest Group in Computational Phonology*.

Hockett, C. F. (1954). Two models of grammatical description. *Morphology: Critical Concepts in Linguistics*, 1:110–138.

Hulden, M. (2009). Foma: a finite-state compiler and library. In *Proceedings of the 12th Conference of the European Chapter of the European Chapter of the Association for Computational Linguistics: Demonstrations Session*, pages 29–32, Athens, Greece. Association for Computational Linguistics.

Hulden, M., Forsberg, M., and Ahlberg, M. (2014). Semi-supervised learning of morphological paradigms and lexicons. In *Proceedings of the 14th Conference of the European Chapter of the Association for Computational Linguistics*, pages 569–578, Gothenburg, Sweden. Association for Computational Linguistics.

Irving, R. W. and Fraser, C. B. (1992). Two algorithms for the longest common subsequence of three (or more) strings. In *Combinatorial Pattern Matching*, pages 214–229. Springer.

Karttunen, L. (2010). Update on finite state morphology tools. *Ms., Palo Alto Research Center.*

Kotus (2007). *Nykysuomen sanalista [Lexicon of modern Finnish]*. Kotus.

Maier, D. (1978). The complexity of some problems on subsequences and supersequences. *Journal of the ACM (JACM)*, 25(2):322–336.

Matthews, P. H. (1972). *Inflectional morphology: A theoretical study based on aspects of Latin verb conjugation*. Cambridge University Press.

Robins, R. H. (1959). In defence of WP. *Transactions of the Philological Society*, 58(1):116–144.

Stump, G. T. (2001). *A theory of paradigm structure*. Cambridge University Press.

Thompson, S. J. (1998). *15,000 Spanish verbs: fully conjugated in all the tenses using pattern verbs*. Center for Innovative Language Learning.

Wang, Q., Pan, M., Shang, Y., and Korkin, D. (2010). A fast heuristic search algorithm for finding the longest common subsequence of multiple strings. In *AAAI Proc.*

Automatic Conversion of Dialectal Tamil Text to Standard Written Tamil Text using FSTs

Marimuthu K
AU-KBC Research Centre,
MIT Campus of Anna University,
Chrompet, Chennai, India.
marimuthuk@live.com

Sobha Lalitha Devi
AU-KBC Research Centre,
MIT Campus of Anna University,
Chrompet, Chennai, India.
sobha@au-kbc.org

Abstract

We present an efficient method to automatically transform spoken language text to standard written language text for various dialects of Tamil. Our work is novel in that it explicitly addresses the problem and need for processing dialectal and spoken language Tamil. Written language equivalents for dialectal and spoken language forms are obtained using Finite State Transducers (FSTs) where spoken language suffixes are replaced with appropriate written language suffixes. Agglutination and compounding in the resultant text is handled using Conditional Random Fields (CRFs) based word boundary identifier. The essential Sandhi corrections are carried out using a heuristic Sandhi Corrector which normalizes the segmented words to simpler sensible words. During experimental evaluations dialectal spoken to written transformer (DSWT) achieved an encouraging accuracy of over 85% in transformation task and also improved the translation quality of Tamil-English machine translation system by 40%. It must be noted that there is no published computational work on processing Tamil dialects. Ours is the first attempt to study various dialects of Tamil in a computational point of view. Thus, the nature of the work reported here is pioneering.

1 Introduction

With the advent of Web 2.0 applications, the focus of communication through the Internet has shifted from publisher oriented activities to user oriented activities such as blogging, social media chats, and discussions in online forums. Given the unmediated nature of these services, users conveniently share the contents in their native languages in a more natural and informal way. This has resulted in bringing together the contents of various languages. More often these contents are informal, colloquial, and dialectal in nature. The dialect is defined as a variety of a language that is distinguished from other varieties of the same language by features of phonology, grammar, and vocabulary and by its use by a group of speakers who are set off from others geographically or socially. The dialectal variation refers to changes in a language due to various influences such as geographic, social, educational, individual and group factors. The dialects vary primarily based on geographical locations. They also vary based on social class, caste, community, gender, etc. which differ phonologically, morphologically, and syntactically (Habash and Rambow, 2006). Here we study spoken and dialectal Tamil language and aim to automatically transform them to standard written language.

Tamil language has more than 70 million speakers worldwide and is spoken mainly in southern India, Sri Lanka, Singapore, and Malaysia. It has 15 known dialects[1] which vary mainly based on geographic location and religious community of the people. The dialects used in southern Tamil Nadu are different from the dialects prevalent in western and other parts of Tamil Nadu. Sri Lankan Tamil is relatively conservative and still retains the older features of Tamil[2]. So its dialect differs considerably from the dialects spoken elsewhere. Tamil dialect is also dependent on religious community. The var-

[1] http://en.wikipedia.org/wiki/Category:Tamil_dialects
[2] www.lmp.ucla.edu

Proceedings of the 2014 Joint Meeting of SIGMORPHON and SIGFSM, pages 37–45,
Baltimore, Maryland USA, June 27 2014. ©2014 Association for Computational Linguistics

iation of dialects based on caste is studied and described by A.K. Ramanujan (1968) where he observed that Tamil Brahmins speak a very distinct form of Tamil known as Brahmin Tamil (BT) which varies greatly from the dialects used in other religious communities. While performing a preliminary corpus study on Tamil dialects, we found that textual contents in personal blogs, social media sites, chat forums, and comments, comprise mostly dialectal and spoken language words similar to what one can hear and use in day-to-day communication. This practice is common because the authors intend to establish a comfortable communication and enhance intimacy with their audiences. This activity produces informal, colloquial and dialectal textual data. These dialectal and spoken language usages will not conform to the standard spellings of Literary Tamil (LT). This causes problems in many text based Natural Language Processing (NLP) systems as they generally work on the assumption that the input is in standard written language. To overcome this problem, these dialectal and spoken language forms need to be converted to Standard Written language Text (SWT) before doing any computational work with them.

Computational processing of dialectal and spoken language Tamil is challenging since the language has motley of dialects and the usage in one dialect varies from other dialects from very minimal to greater extents. It is also very likely that multiple spoken-forms of a given word within a dialect which we call as '**variants**' may correspond to single canonical written-form word and a spoken-form word may map to more than one canonical written-form. These situations exist in all Tamil dialects. In addition, it is very likely to encounter conflicts with the spoken and written-forms of one dialect with other dialects and vice versa. Most importantly, the dialects are used mainly in spoken communication and when they are written by users, they do not conform to standard spoken-form spellings and sometimes inconsistent spellings are used even for a single written-form of a word. In other words Schiffman (1988) noted that every usage of a given spoken-form can be considered as Standard Spoken Tamil (SST) unless it has wrong spellings to become nonsensical.

Few researchers have attempted to transform the dialects and spoken-forms of languages to standard written languages. Habash and Rambow (2006) developed MAGEAD, a morphological analyzer and generator for Arabic dialects where the authors made use of *root+pattern+features* representation for the transformation of Arabic dialects to Modern Standard Arabic (MSA) and performed morphological analysis. In the case of Tamil language, Umamaheswari et al. (2011) proposed a technique based on pattern mapping and spelling variation rules for transforming colloquial words to written-language words. The reported work considered only a handful of rules for the most common spoken forms. So this approach will fail when dialectal variants of words are encountered because it is more likely that the spelling variation rules of the spoken language vary from the rules of dialectal usages. This limitation hinders the possibility of the system to generalize. Alternatively, performing a simple list based mapping between spoken and written form words is also inefficient and unattainable.

Spoken language words exhibit fairly regular pattern of suffixations and inflections within a given paradigm (Schiffman, 1999). So we propose a novel method based on Finite State Transducers for effectively transforming dialectal and spoken Tamil to standard written Tamil. We make use of the regularity of suffixations and model them as FSTs. These FSTs are used to perform transformation which produces words in standard literary Tamil.

Our experimental results show that DSWT achieves high precision and recall values. In addition, it improves the translation quality of machine translation systems when unknown words occur mainly due to colloquialism. This improvement gradually increases as the unknown word rate increases due to colloquial and dialectal nature of words.

Broadly, DSWT can be used in a variety of NLP applications such as Morphological Analysis, Rule-based and Statistical Machine Translation (SMT), Information Retrieval (IR), Named-Entity Recognition (NER), and Text-To-Speech (TTS). In general, it can be used in any NLP system where there is a need to retrieve written language words from dialectal and spoken language Tamil words.

The paper is further organized as follows: In section 2, the challenges in processing Tamil dialects are explained. Section 3 explains the corpus collection and study. Section 4 explains the peculiarities seen in spoken and dialectal Tamil. Section 5 introduces the system architecture of DSWT. Section 6 describes conducted Experimental evaluations and the results. Section 7 discusses about the results and the paper concludes with a conclusion section.

2 Challenges in Processing Tamil Dialects

Tamil, a member of Dravidian language family, is highly inflectional and agglutinative in nature. The phenomenon of agglutination becomes much pronounced in dialects and spoken-form communication where much of the phonemes of suffixes get truncated and form agglutinated words which usually have two or more simpler words in them. A comprehensive study on the *Grammar of Spoken Tamil* for various syntactic categories is presented in Schiffman (1979) and Schiffman (1999). Various dialects are generally used in spoken discourse and while writing them people use inconsistent spellings for a given spoken language word. The spelling usages primarily depend on educational qualification of the authors. Sometimes, the authors intentionally use certain types of spelling to express satire and humor.

Due to this spelling and dialectal variation many-to-one mapping happens where all the variants correspond to single canonical written form. This is illustrated with the dialectal and spelling variants of the verb "paarkkiReen" (see) in Fig 1.

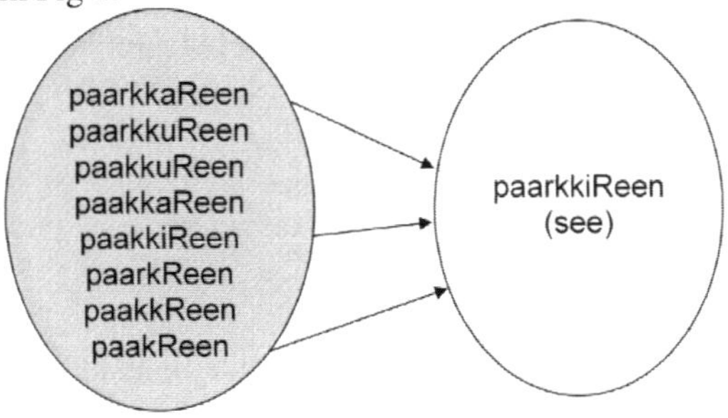

Figure 1. many-to-one mapping

For the words that belong to the above case, there is no hard rule that a particular pattern of spelling will be used and referred to while the text is written by people. In addition to this mapping, one-to-many mapping is also possible where a single spoken form maps to multiple canonical written forms.

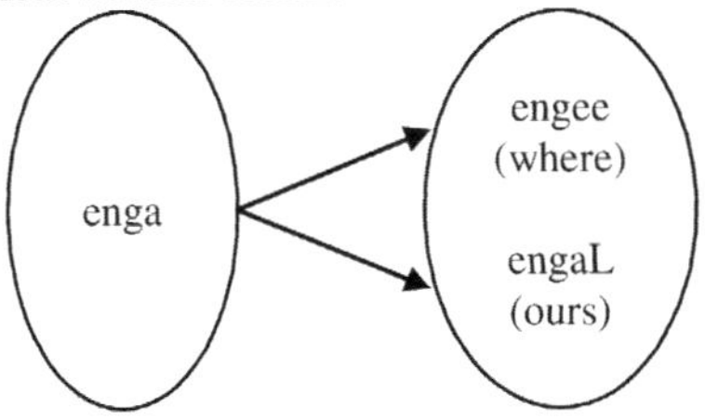

Figure 2. one-to-many mapping

In the case of one-to-many mapping, multiple written language words will be obtained. Choosing a correct written language word over other words is dependent on the context where the dialectal spoken language word occurs. In some cases, the sentence may be terminated by punctuations such as question marks which can be made use of to select an appropriate written language word. To achieve correct selection of a word, an extensive study has to be conducted and is not the focus of this paper. In the current work we are interested in obtaining as many possible mappings as possible. Many-to-one mapping occurs mainly due to dialectal and spelling variations of spoken-forms whereas one-to-many mapping happens because a single spoken-form may convey different meanings in different contexts. Dialectal spoken forms of many-to-one and one-to-many mappings are more prevalent than one-to-one mapping where a dialectal spoken form maps to exactly one written form word.

3 Data Collection and Corpus Study

The dialectal spoken form of a language is primarily used for colloquial and informal communication among native speakers. They are also commonly seen in personal blogs, social media chats and comments, discussion forums etc. Given this informal nature of the language usage, such a variety is not used in formal print and broadcasting media as they mainly use standard literary Tamil.

In our preliminary study, we found that textual contents in personal blogs, tweets, and chats have significantly large number of dialectal and spoken language words than those are found in other standard online resources such as news publishers, entertainment media websites etc.

Since we focus on processing various Tamil dialects and their spoken language variants, we have collected publicly available data from the above mentioned online resources for this work.

The collected data belongs to authors from various geographic locations where different Tamil dialects exist. The textual contents in the selected resources mainly contain movie reviews, narratives, travel experiences, fables, poems, and sometimes an informal discourse, all in a casual and colloquial manner. Further, we were able to collect variants of spoken forms which vary with respect to person, social status, location, community, gender, age, qualification etc.

Though Tamil language has 15 dialects, in this work, we focused only on 5 dialects namely, Central Tamil dialect, Madurai Tamil, Tirunelveli Tamil, Brahmin Tamil, Kongu Tamil and common spoken language forms. In Table 1, we present the corpus distribution with respect to the dialects and the number of dialectal and spoken language words.

Name of the Tamil Dialect	No. of Dialectal words
Central Tamil dialect	584
Madurai Tamil	864
Tirunelveli Tamil	2074
Brahmin Tamil	2286
Kongu Tamil	910
Common Spoken Forms	5810

Table 1. Corpus distribution among dialects

We performed an in-depth study on the collected data and found some peculiarities which exist in some dialects. Some of the observed peculiarities are described in Section 4.

4 Tamil Dialects and their Peculiarities

Some dialectal words have totally different meaning in SST and in other dialects or in standard literary Tamil. For instance, consider the following dialectal sentence (Tirunelveli Tamil)

ela, inga vaala.
Hey here come
'Hey come here!'

The words "*ela*" and "*vaala*" convey different meanings in different contexts and dialects. In SST they denote "*leaf*" and "*tail*" respectively while in Tirunelveli Tamil dialect they convey the meaning "*hey*" and "*come*" respectively.

Though these ambiguities are resolved when the context is considered, they make the transformation task challenging since this is a word-level task and no context information is taken into account during transformation.

The example in table 2, illustrates spelling based variants where the variants map to single canonical written form. We observed that the most common form of spoken-language usage is the use and representation of "*enRu*" (ADV) as four variants which are shown in Table 2.

Spoken form Variants	Written form Equivalent
[Noun/Pronoun/Verb] + "nu"	[Noun/Pronoun/Verb] + "enRu"
[Noun/Pronoun/Verb] + "nnu"	[Noun/Pronoun/Verb] + "enRu"
[Noun/Pronoun/Verb] + "unu"	[Noun/Pronoun/Verb] + "enRu"
[Noun/Pronoun/Verb] + "unnu"	[Noun/Pronoun/Verb] + "enRu"

Table 2. Spoken variants and written language

The dialectal variants of the verb "*vanthaarkaL*" (they came) is illustrated in table 3.

Dialectal variants	Written form Equivalent
[Verb] + "aaka"	[Verb] + "aarkaL"
[Verb] + "aangka"	[Verb] + "aarkaL"

Table 3. Dialectal variants & written language

It can be observed from Table 3 that the dialectal suffixes vary from each other but they all map to same written form suffix. Despite the dialectal variation, they all convey the same meaning. But they vary syntactically. The "*aaka*" suffix functions as adverbial marker in standard literary Tamil whereas it acts as person, number, gender (PNG) marker in Madurai Tamil dialect.

5 System Architecture

In this section we describe our system architecture which is depicted in Figure 3. Our dialectal spoken to written transformer (DSWT) has three main components namely, Transformation Engine, CRF word boundary identifier and heuristic Sandhi corrector.

- Transformation Engine contains FSTs for the dialectal and spoken language to standard written language transformation. The resultant words may be agglutinated and is decomposed with the help of CRF boundary identifier.
- CRF Word Boundary Identifier module identifies the word boundaries in agglutinated words and splits them into a set of constituent simpler words.
- Heuristic Sandhi Corrector module makes necessary spelling changes to the segmented constituent words and standardizes them to canonical and meaningful simpler words.

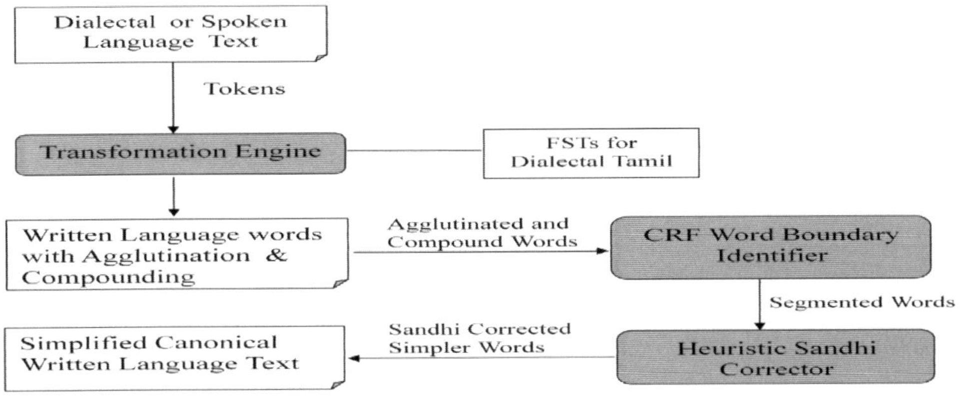

Figure 3. System Architecture

5.1 Transformation Engine

The function of Transformation engine is to transform dialectal and spoken language words into standardized literary Tamil words, similar to the official form of Tamil that is used in government publications such as official memorandums, news and print media, and formal political speeches.

Modeling FSTs for Transformation

Given the regular pattern of inflections within a paradigm, we use paradigm based approach for the variation modeling. Specifically, the dialectal usages, spoken language forms and their variants are modeled as *"root+spoken-language-suffix"* where it will get transformed into *"root+written-language-suffix"* after transformation. We had used *AT&T's FSM library*[3] for generating FSTs. The FST shown in Fig. 4 shows the state transitions for some spoken language words.

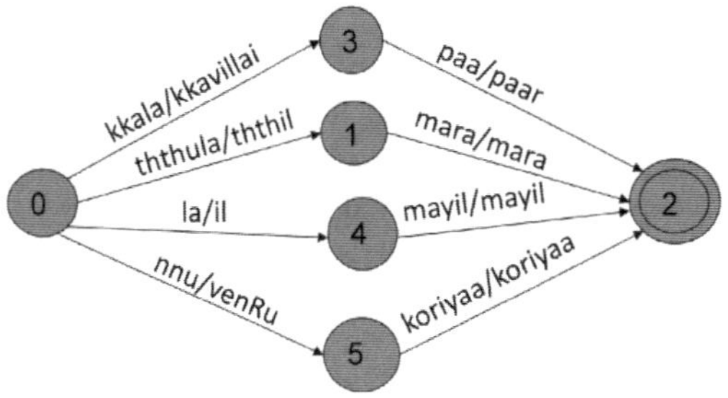

Figure 4. Sample FST

It can be observed from Figure 4 that spoken and dialectal words are processed in right to left fashion. This way of processing is adopted since the number of unique suffixation is few when compared to the number of root words. This will make the suffix matching faster and hence achieves quick transformation. This makes FSTs as an efficient tool for dialectal or variation modeling.

Algorithm for Transformation

The algorithm that is used to transform dialectal and spoken language text is given below.

```
for each dialectal/spoken-language word
  check possible suffixations in FST
    for each suffixation
      if FST accepts & generates written
         language equivalents for all suffixes
        return (root + written-language-suffix)
      else
        return dialectal/spoken-language-word
for each agglutinated & compound word
  do CRF word boundary identification
    for each constituent word (CW)
      do Sandhi Correction
        return simple constituent words
```

5.2 Decomposition of Agglutinated and Compound Words using CRF

Since Tamil is a morphologically rich language, the phenomenon of agglutination and compounding in standard written language Tamil is high and very common. It is also present in dialectal and spoken language Tamil. This poses a number of challenges to the development of NLP systems. To solve these challenges, we segment the agglutinated and compound words into simpler constituent words. This decomposition is achieved using two components namely

[3] http://www2.research.att.com/~fsmtools/fsm/

Agglutinated word or Compound Word	Boundary Identification and Word Segmentation	Sandhi Correction Functions			
		No Change	Insertion	Deletion	Substitution
nampuvathillaiyenRu (will not be believing)	nampuvath illai yenRu	illai	nampuvathu	enRu	
muththokuppukaLutaya (comprising of three volumes)	muth thokuppukaL utaya	thokuppukaL utaya			muu

Table 4. Boundary identification and Sandhi Correction

Table 4 clearly manifests the boundary of a constituent word within a compound or an agglutinated word which may contain one or more word-boundaries. It is observed that for "**n**" constituent words in a compound or an agglutinated word, there exists exactly (**n-1**) shared word-boundaries where (**n>0**).

CRF word boundary identifier and *Heuristic Sandhi Corrector*. We have developed the word boundary identifier for boundary identification and segmentation as described in Marimuthu et al. (2013) and heuristic rule based Sandhi corrector for making spelling changes to the segmented words.

CRF Word-Boundary Identifier

CRF based word-boundary identifier marks the boundaries of simpler constituent words in agglutinated and compound words and segments them. CRFs are a discriminative probabilistic framework for labeling and segmenting sequential data. They are undirected graphical models trained to maximize a conditional probability (Lafferty et al., 2001).

Generally word-boundary identification is studied extensively for languages such as Chinese and Japanese but the necessity for Indian languages was not considered until recently. Although there is no standard definition of word-boundary in Chinese, Peng et al. (2004) describe a robust approach for Chinese word segmentation using linear-chain CRFs where the flexibility of CRFs to support arbitrary overlapping features with long-range dependencies and multiple levels of granularity are utilized by integrating the rich domain knowledge in the form of multiple lexicons of characters and words into the framework for accurate word segmentation.

In case of Japanese, though the word boundaries are not clear, Kudo et al. (2004) used CRFs for Japanese morphological analysis where they show how CRFs can be applied to situations where word-boundary ambiguity exists.

Marimuthu et al. (2013) worked on word boundary identification and segmentation in Tamil where they model the boundary identification as a sequence labeling task [i.e. a tagging task]. The absence of word-boundary ambiguity in Tamil language favors the boundary identification task and predominantly eliminates the need for providing further knowledge to CRFs such as multiple lexicons as in the case of Chinese word segmentation. Hence we have used word level features alone for training the CRFs.

Sandhi Correction using Word-level Contextual Rules

Word-level contextual rules are the spelling rules in which each constituent word of an agglutinated or compound word is dependent either on the previous or the next or both constituent words to give a correct meaning.

After boundary identification, suppose an agglutinated or a compound word is split into three constituent words, Sandhi correction for the first constituent word is dependent only on the second constituent word while the second word's Sandhi correction depends on both first and third constituent word whereas the third constituent word's Sandhi correction depends on second constituent word alone.

Sandhi correction is performed using these rules to make necessary spelling changes to the boundary-segmented words in order to normalize them to sensible simpler words. It is accomplished using three tasks namely insertion, deletion, and substitution as described in Marimuthu et al. (2013).

For instance, after boundary identification the word *"nampuvathillaiyenRu" (will not be believing)* will be boundary marked and Sandhi corrected as shown in the Table 4 above.

Advantages of Word boundary Identification

Morphological Analysis of simpler words is much easier than analyzing agglutinated and compound words.

Tamil Dialects	No. of dialectal words	Precision (%)	Recall (%)	F-Measure (%)
Central Tamil dialect	584	88.0	89.3	88.6
Madurai Tamil	864	85.2	87.5	85.3
Tirunelveli Tamil	2074	83.4	88.6	85.9
Brahmin Tamil	2286	87.3	89.5	88.4
Kongu Tamil	910	89.1	90.4	89.7
Common Spoken Forms	5810	86.0	88.3	87.1

Table 5. Direct Evaluation Results

So the word-boundary identifier eases the task of morphological analyzer in identifying the individual morphemes. In addition, it nullifies the unknown words category if it occurs due to agglutination and compounding. As a result, it improves the recall of the morphological analyzer and any advanced NLP system. For example, with Tamil, SMT models usually perform better when the compound words are broken into their components. This 'segmentation' gives the word alignment greater resolution when matching the groupings between the two languages.

6 Experimental Evaluation

Here we perform evaluation of the performance of DSWT with test corpus of 12528 words. We perform two types of evaluations: direct and indirect evaluation.

In direct evaluation, we evaluate the system using gold standard. In indirect evaluation the system is evaluated using machine translation application. The aim in indirect evaluation is to understand the effect of dialectal and spoken language transformation in machine translation.

6.1 Direct Evaluation

We evaluate DSWT performance using the standard evaluation metrics: Precision, Recall, and F-measure. Precision and Recall values are calculated separately for each dialect using a gold standard. They are calculated using the cases described below:

A: The dialectal or spoken language transformation yields one or many correct standard written language words.
B: The dialectal or spoken language transformation yields at least one correct standard written language word.
C: The dialectal or spoken language transformation yields no output.
D: Number of dialectal or spoken language words given as input.

Precision is then calculated as: A/(D-C)
Recall is calculated as: (A+B)/D
F-Measure is the harmonic mean of *Precision* and *Recall.*
The obtained results for the considered 5 Tamil dialects and common spoken language forms are summarized in Table 5 above.

6.2 Indirect Evaluation

For indirect evaluation, we had used DSWT with Google Translate (GT) to measure the influence of DSWT in Tamil-English machine translation, and evaluated the improvement.

Our test data had 100 Tamil sentences which are of dialectal and colloquial in nature. At first, we used GT to translate these sentences to English. This is Output1. Then we used our DSWT to transform the dialectal sentences into standard written Tamil. After this, the standard sentences were translated to English using GT. This corresponds to Output2.

We then performed subjective evaluations of Output1 and Output2 with the help of three native Tamil speakers whose second language is English. The three evaluation scores for each sentence in Output1 and Output2 are averaged. The obtained scores are shown in Table 6.

Subjective Evaluation Scores before dialectal Transformation		**Subjective Evaluation Scores after dialectal Transformation**	
No. of sentences	*Achieved Scores*	*No. of Sentences*	*Achieved Scores*
20	0	4	0
70	1	14	1
8	2	28	2
2	3	30	3
0	4	24	4

Table 6. Subjective evaluation results

We used a scoring scale of 0-4 where
0 → no translation happened.

Before performing Dialectal Transformation Task		After performing Dialectal Transformation Task	
Dialectal Spoken Tamil	*Google Translate results*	*Standardized Written Tamil*	*Google Translate results*
ஒடனே வந்துரு. (otanee vanthuru)	vanturu otane. (✗)	உடனே வந்துவிடு. (utanee vanthuvitu)	Come immediately. (✓)
ஒடனே வந்துருல. (otanee vanthurula)	vanturula otane. (✗)	உடனே வந்துவிடு. (utanee vanthuvitu)	Come immediately. (✓)
அவங்க வந்தாங்க. (avanga vanthaanga)	she had come. (?)	அவர்கள் வந்தார்கள். (avarkaL vanthaarkaL)	They came. (✓)
அவுக வந்தாக. (avuka vanthaaka)	avuka to come. (✗)	அவர்கள் வந்தார்கள். (avarkaL vanthaarkaL)	They came. (✓)

Table 7. Tamil-English Google Translate results before and after dialectal text transformation

Sentences marked as (✗) are incorrectly translated into English and those that are marked as (?) may be partially correct. The sentences that are marked as (✔) are the correct English translations.

1 → lexical translation of few words happen and no meaning can be inferred from the translation output.

2 → complete lexical translations happen and some meaning can be inferred from the translation output.

3 → meaning can be inferred from translation output but contains some grammatical errors.

4 → complete meaning is understandable with very minor errors.

It can be observed from the results in Table 6 that GT failed to translate dialectal and spoken language sentences. But the failure got mitigated after transformation causing dramatic improvement in translation quality. The following Table illustrates few examples where the translation quality has improved after transforming dialectal spoken language.

It must be noted from Table 7 that after the transformation of dialectal spoken language, all the sentences were able to achieve their English equivalents during machine translation. This suggests that almost all word categories in Tamil can achieve improved translations if the words are given as standard simple written language words. This experiment emphasizes the importance of feeding the machine translation systems with standard written language text to achieve quality translations and better results.

7 Results and Discussion

We observe that the achieved accuracy is higher for Kongu Tamil dialect when compared to other dialects. This is because words in this dialect are rarely polysemous in nature. But the number of polysemous words is high in the case of Madurai and Tirunelveli Tamil dialect and this resulted in low accuracy of transformation.

While performing transformation, the possible causes for ending up with unknown words may be due to the absence of suffix patterns in FSTs, errors in input words, uncommonly transliterated words, and English acronyms. The standard written language words convey a particular meaning in standard literary Tamil and completely different meaning in dialectal usages. For instance, consider the verb "*vanthaaka*". In standard literary Tamil, this is used in the imperative sense "*should come*" while in Tirunelveli Tamil dialect it is used in the sense "*somebody came*".

8 Conclusion and Future Work

We have presented a dialectal and spoken language to standard written language transformer for Tamil language and evaluated its performance directly using standard evaluation metrics and indirectly using Google Translate for Tamil to English machine translation. The achieved results are encouraging.

There is no readily available corpus for processing dialectal and spoken Tamil texts and we have collected the dialectal and spoken language corpus for developmental and evaluation tasks. This corpus can be made use of for developing other NLP applications.

In case of one-to-many mapping, multiple written language forms will be emitted as outputs. Hence, determining which written-form of word to be adopted over other resultant written-forms has to be done based on the meaning of the whole sentence in which the spoken-language word occurs. This will be the focus of our future direction of the work.

References

A. K. Ramanujan. 1968. *Spoken and Written Tamil, the verb*. University of Chicago. Pages 74.

Fuchun Peng, Fangfang Feng and Andrew McCallum. 2004.*Chinese Segmentation and New Word Detection using Conditional Random Fields*, Computer Science Department Faculty Publication Series. Paper 92. University of Massachusetts – Amherst.

Harold F. Schiffman. 1979. *A Grammar of Spoken Tamil,* Christian Literature Society, Madras, India. Pp. i-viii, 1-104.

Harold F. Schiffman. 1988. *Standardization or restandardization: The case for "Standard" Spoken Tamil*, Language in Society, Cambridge University Press, United States of America. Pages 359-385.

Harold F. Schiffman. 1999. *A Reference Grammar of Spoken Tamil,* Cambridge University Press, Pp. i-xxii,1-232.

J. Lafferty, A. McCallum, and F. Pereira. 2001. *Conditional Random Fields: Probabilistic Models for Segmenting and Labeling Sequence Data.* In Proceedings of the 18th International Conference on Machine Learning, pages 282–289.

Marimuthu K., Amudha K., Bakiyavathi T. and Sobha Lalitha Devi. 2013. *Word Boundary Identifier as a Catalyzer and Performance Booster for Tamil Morphological Analyzer*, in proceedings of 6th Language and Technology Conference, Human Language Technologies as a challenge for Computer Science and Linguistics, Poznan, Poland.

Milton Singer and Bernard S. Cohn. 2007. *The Structure of Variation: A Study in Caste Dialects*, Structure and Change in Indian Society, University of Chicago, Chapter 19, pages 461-470.

Nizar Habash and Owen Rambow. 2006. *MAGEAD: A Morphological Analyzer and Generator for the Arabic Dialects*, In proceedings of the 21st International Conference on Computational Linguistics and 44th Annual Meeting of the ACL, Sydney, Australia. Pages 681-688

Sajib Dasgupta and Vincent Ng. 2007. *Unsupervised Word Segmentation for Bangla*, In proceedings of the Fifth International Conference on Natural Language Processing(ICON), Hyderabad, India.

Taku Kudo, Kaoru Yamamoto and Yuji Matsumoto. 2004. *Applying Conditional Random Fields to Japanese Morphological Analysis*, In proceedings of Empirical Methods on Natural Language Processing, Barcelona, Spain.

Umamaheswari E, Karthika Ranganathan, Geetha TV, Ranjani Parthasarathi, and Madhan Karky. 2011. *Enhancement of Morphological Analyzer with compound, numeral and colloquial word handler*, Proceedings of ICON-2011: 9th International Conference on Natural Language Processing, Macmillan Publishers, India.

Rule Based Morphological Analyzer of Kazakh Language

Gulshat Kessikbayeva
Hacettepe University, Department of Computer Engineering,
Ankara,Turkey
shatik2030@gmail.com

Ilyas Cicekli
Hacettepe University, Department of Computer Engineering,
Ankara,Turkey
ilyas@cs.hacettepe.edu.tr

Abstract

Having a morphological analyzer is a very critical issue especially for NLP related tasks on agglutinative languages. This paper presents a detailed computational analysis of Kazakh language which is an agglutinative language. With a detailed analysis of Kazakh language morphology, the formalization of rules over all morphotactics of Kazakh language is worked out and a rule-based morphological analyzer is developed for Kazakh language. The morphological analyzer is constructed using two-level morphology approach with Xerox finite state tools and some implementation details of rule-based morphological analyzer have been presented in this paper.

1 Introduction

Kazakh language is a Turkic language which belongs to Kipchak branch of Ural-Altaic language family and it is spoken approximately by 8 million people. It is the official language of Kazakhstan and it has also speakers in Russia, China, Mongolia, Iran, Turkey, Afghanistan and Germany. It is closely related to other Turkic languages and there exists mutual intelligibility among them. Words in Kazakh language can be generated from root words recursively by adding proper suffixes. Thus, Kazakh language has agglutinative form and has vowel harmony property except for loan-words from other languages such as Russian, Persian and Arabic.

Having a morphological analyzer for an agglutinative language is a starting point for Natural Language Processing (NLP) related researches. An analysis of inflectional affixes of Kazakh language is studied within the work of a Kazakh segmentation system (Altenbek and Wang, 2010). A finite state approach for Kazakh nominals is presented (Kairakbay and Zaurbekov, 2013) and it only gives specific alternation rules without generalized forms of alternations. Here we present all generalized forms of all alternation rules. Moreover, many studies and researches have been done upon on morphological analysis of Turkic languages (Altintas and Cicekli, 2001; Oflazer, 1994; Coltekin, 2010; Tantug et al., 2006; Orhun et al, 2009). However there is no complete work which provides a detailed computational analysis of Kazakh language morphology and this paper tries to do that.

The organization of the rest of the paper is as follows. Next section gives a brief comparison of Kazakh language and Turkish morphologies. Section 3 presents Kazakh vowel and consonant harmony rules. Then, nouns with their inflections are presented in Section 4. Section 4 also presents morphotactic rules for nouns, pronouns, adjectives, adverbs and numerals. The detailed morphological structure of verbs is introduced in Section 5. Results of the performed tests are presented together with their analysis in Section 6. At last, conclusion and future work are described in Section 7.

2 Comparison of Closely Related Languages

There are many studies and researches prior made on closely related languages by comparing them for many purposes related with NLP such as Turkish–Crimean Tatar (Altintas and Cicekli, 2001), Turkish–Azerbaijani (Hamzaoğlu, 1993), Turkish–Turkmen (Tantuğ et al., 2007), Turkish-Uygur (Orhun et al, 2009) and Tatar-Kazakh (Salimzyanov et al, 2013). A deep comparison of Kazakh and Turkish languages from computational view is another study which is in out of scope for this work. However, in this study, a brief grammatical comparison of these languages is given in order to give a better analysis of Kazakh language.

Proceedings of the 2014 Joint Meeting of SIGMORPHON and SIGFSM, pages 46–54,
Baltimore, Maryland USA, June 27 2014.

Kazakh and Turkish languages have many common parts due to being in same language family. Possible differences are mostly morpheme based rather than deep grammar differences. Distinct morphemes can be added in order to get same meaning. There exist some differences in their alphabets, their vowel and consonant harmony rules, their possessive forms of nouns, and inflections of verbs as given in Table 1. There are extra 9 letters in Kazakh alphabet, and Kazakh alphabet also has 4 additional letters for Russian loan words.

Both Kazakh language and Turkish employ vowel harmony rules when morphemes are added. Vowel harmony is defined according to last morpheme containing back or front vowel. In Kazakh language, if the last morpheme contains a back vowel then the vowel of next coming suffix is *a* or *ı*. If the last morpheme contains one of front vowels then the vowel of next coming suffix is *e* or *i*. In Turkish, suffixes with vowels *a*, *ı*, *u* follow morphemes with vowels *a*, *o*, *u*, *ı* and suffixes with vowels *e*, *i*, *ü* follow morphemes with vowels *e*, *i*, *ü*, *ö* depending on being rounded and unrounded vowels. Consonant harmony rule related with voiceless letters is similar in both languages.

	Turkish	Kazakh Language
Alphabet	Latin 29 letters (8 Vowels, 21 Consonant)	Cyril 42 letters (10 Vowels, 25 Consonants, 3 Compound Letters, 4 Russian Loan Word Letters)
Vowel & Consonant Harmony	Synharmonism according to back, front, unrounded and rounded vowels	Synharmonism according to back and front vowels
Possessive Forms of Nouns	6 types of possessive agreements	8 types of possessive agreements
Case Forms of Nouns	7 Case Forms	7 Case Forms
Verbs	Similar Tenses	Similar Tenses

Table 1. Comparison of Kazakh and Turkish.

In Kazakh language there are 8 types of personal possessive agreement morphemes as given in Table 2. Kazakh language has two additional possessive agreements for second person.

There are some identical tenses and moods of verbs in both language such as definite past tense, present tense, imperative mood, optative mood and conditional mood. They have nearly same morphemes for tenses. On the other hand there are some tenses of verbs which are identical according to meaning and usage, but different morphemes are used. Moreover, in Kazakh language there are some tenses such as goal oriented future and present tenses which do not exist in Turkish language.

Possessive Pronoun	Representation		Examples for Eke, "father"	
None Possessive	Pnon		Eke	father
My	P1Sg	1	Eke-m	my father
Your	P2Sg	2	Eke-N	your father
Your (Polite)	P2PSg	2	Eke-Niz	your father
His/Her	P3Sg	3	Eke-si	his father
Our	P1Pl	1	Eke-miz	our father
Your Plural	P2Pl	2	Eke-leriN	your father
Your Plural (Polite)	P2PPl	2	Eke-leriNiz	your father
Their	P3Pl	3	Eke-leri	their father

Table 2. Possessive Agreement of Nouns.

3 Vowel and Consonant Harmony

Kazakh is officially written in the Cyrillic alphabet. In its history, it was represented by Arabic, Latin and Cyrillic letters. Nowadays switching back to Latin alphabets in 20 years is planned by the Kazakh government. In the beginning stage of study, Latin transcription of Cyril version is used for convenience.

Two main issues of language such as morphotactics and alternations can be dealt with Xerox tools. First of all, morphotactic rules are represented by encoding a finite-state network. Then, a finite-state transducer for alternations is constructed. Then, the formed network and the transducer are composed into a single final network which cover all morphological aspects of the language such as morphemes, derivations, inflections, alternations and geminations (Beesley and Karttunen, 2003).

Vowel harmony of Kazakh language obeys a rule such that vowels in each syllable should match according to being front or back vowel. It is called synharmonism and it is basic linguistic structure of nearly all Turkic languages (Demirci, 2006). For example, a word *qa-la-lar-dIN,* "of cities" has a stem *qa-la*, "city" and two syllables of containing back vowels according to the vowel harmony rule. Here *–lar* is an affix of Plural form and *–dIN* is an affix of Genitive case. However, as stated before, there are a lot of loan words from Persian and generally they do not obey vowel harmony rules. For example, a word *mu-Ga-lim,* "teacher" has first two syllables have back vowels and the last one has a front vowel. So suffixes to be added are defined according to the last syllable. For example, a word *muGalim-der-diN*, "of teachers" has suffixes with front vowels. On the other hand, there are morphemes with static front vowels which are independently from the type of last syllable can be added to all words such as Instrumental suffix *–men*. In this case, all suffixes added after that should contain front vowels.

Name	XFST	Type 1	Type 2
Sonorous Consonant	SCons	**l r y w**	**m n N**
Voiced Consonant	VCons	**z Z**	**b v g d**
Voiceless Consonant	VLCons	**p f q k t s S C x c**	
Consonant	Cons	**b p t c x d r z Z s S C G f q k g N l m n h w y v**	
Vowel	Vowel	**a e E i I O o u U j**	
Front Vowel	FVowel	**e E i O U j**	
Back Vowel	BVowel	**a I o u**	

Table 3. Groups of Kazakh letters according to their sound. Upper case letters are used for non-Latin letters.

In order to construct a finite-state transducer for alternation rules, there are some capital letters such as *A, J, H, B, P, C, D, Q, K, T* are defined in intermediate level and they are invisible by user. These representations are used for substitution such as *A* is for *a* and *e* and *J* is for *I* and *i*. So if suffix *dA* should be added according to morphotactic rules, it means suffixes *da* or *de* should be considered. In Table 3, there are group of letters defined according to their sounds and these groups are used in alternation rules (Valyaeva, 2007).

Consonant harmony rules are varied according to the last letter of a word with in morphotactic rules. As in Table 3, different patterns are presented in order to visualize the relation between common valid rules and to generalize morphotactic rules. Thus, in each case according to morphotactic rules there are proper alternation rules for morphemes.

GROUP 1					
Ablative Case		Locative case		Dative Case	
dAn		dA		TA	
tAn		tA		TA	
nAn	3	ndA	3	nA	3
				A	1/2
GROUP 2					
Genitive Case		Accusative Case		Poss. Affix-2	
dJN		dJ		diki	
tJN		tJ		tiki	
nJN	3	nJ		niki	
		n	3		
GROUP 3					
Plural Form of Noun		Negative Form		A1Pl	
dAr	1	bA		bJz	
tAr		pA		pJz	
lAr	r y w	mA		mJz	
GROUP 4					
Instrumental Case				A1Sg	
ben				bJn	
pen				pJn	
men	3			mJn	

Table 4. Alternation rules according to groups of letters.

All alternation rules for suffixes depend on the last letter of a morpheme with in morphotactic rules and Table 4 gives some groupings that can be made in order to set some generalized rules overall. Patterns of last letters of morphemes in Table 4 are matched with groups of letters presented in Table 3. In Table 4, Locative case affix is *–dA*, if the last letter of a morpheme is one of Vowel, Sonorous

Consonant or Voiced Consonant of Type 1 in Table 3. On the other hand, it is *–tA*, if the last letter is Voiceless Consonant or Voiced Consonant of Type 2. Here *A* is for *a* or *e* according to last syllable of containing Front or Back Vowel.

In Table 4, boxes presented by numbers such as 1, 2 and 3 are used for personal possessive agreements in Table 2. For example, word *Eke*, "father" in Ablative case without a possessive agreement takes suffix *–den*, because the word *Eke* ends with vowel *e*. However, in third person possessive agreement it takes suffix *–nen*, because all words with third person possessive agreement in Ablative case always take suffix *–nen* even though the third person possessive agreement morpheme ends with vowel.

According to those similarities in Table 4, there are some generalized rules which are valid in many cases in grammar including verbs and derivations. Some of these generalized rules derived from close patterns given in Table 4, are given in Table 5. For example, Rule 12 in Table 5 represents rules for Locative and Dative cases in Group 1 in Table 4. In Table 4, Locative and Dative suffix rules are nearly identical and have same patterns which can be observed visually. Also, Accusative and Possessive Pronouns of Type 2 are same.

	1	2
1	**Rule 11** *Ablative Case*	**Rule 12** *Locative, Dative cases*
2	**Rule 21** *Genitive case*	**Rule 22** *Accusative case, Poss. Affix-2*
3	**Rule 31** *Plural Form of Noun*	**Rule 32** *Negation, Personal Agreement of A1Pl*
4	**Rule 41** *Instrumental case*	**Rule 42** *Personal Agreement of A1Sg*

Table 5. Generalized Rules.

In Dative case of GROUP 1 in Table 4, if the last letter is Back Vowel then *T* is replaced by *G* and *T* is replaced by *g* if the last letter is Front Vowel. Thus, a word *bala*, "child" becomes *bala-Ga*, "to child" and a word *Eke*, "father" will be *Eke-ge*, "to father". If the last letter is Voiceless Consonant, *T* is replaced by *q* or *k* depending on whether the last syllable contains Back Vowel or Front Vowel. For example, a word *kitap-qa*, "to book" has the last letter of Voiceless Consonant and the last syllable contains Back Vowel, thus *T* is replaced by *q*. A word *mektep-ke*, "to school" has the last letter of Voiceless Consonant and the last syllable contains Front vowel, thus *T* is replaced by *k*.

After detailed analysis of the language it can be seen that there are mainly common rules of alternations valid over all grammar. There are about 25 main alternation rules defined for all system together with generalized rules and 7 exception rules for each case. All these rules are implemented with XFST tools (Beesley and Karttunen, 2003). For instance, some mainly used common rules are given below and they are called by capital letters defined only in intermediate level. As mentioned before they are invisible by user. Here 0 is for empty character.

Rule H & Rule B: *H* is realized as 0 or *J*, *B* is realized as 0 or *A*.

```
[H->0,B->0||[Vowel]%+_[Cons]]
[H->J,B->A]
```

If the last letter of a morpheme is Vowel and the first letter of the following suffix is Consonant then *H* and *B* are realized as 0. Otherwise, they are realized as *J* and *B*. Some examples are:

ana-Hm→ *ana-m*, "my mother"
iS-Hm→ iS-Jm→Rule J→*iSim*, "my stomache"
ege-Br→ *ege-r*, "will sharpen"
bar-Br→ bar-Ar→ Rule A→*bar-ar*, "will go"

Rule J & Rule A: *J* is realized as *I* or *i* and *A* is realized as *y*, *a* or *e*.

```
[A->y||[Vowel]%+_]
[A->a,J->I||[BVowel](Cons)*%+?*_]
[A->e,J->i||[FVowel](Cons)*%+?*_]
```

If the last letter of a morpheme is Vowel then *A* is realized as *y*, and if the last syllable of a morpheme contains Back Vowel then *A* and *J* are realized as *a* and *I*. Otherwise, if the last syllable of a morpheme contains Front Vowel then *A* and *J* are realized as *e* and *i*. Some examples are:

bas-Hm→bas-Jm→*basIm*, "my head"
dos-tAr→*dos-tar*, "friends"
dEpter-lAr→ *dEpter-ler*, "copybooks"
barma-AmIn→*barma-ymIn*, "I will not go"

Rule T (a part of Rule 12 in Table 5)**:** *T* is realized as *q*, *G*, *k* or *g*.

```
[T->q||[BVowel](?)[VLCons]%+_]
[T->k||[FVowel](?)[VLCons]%+_]
[T->G||[BVowel](?)[0|SCons|VCons1]%+_]
[T->g||[FVowel](?)[0|SCons|VCons1]%+_]
```

This rule is a part of Rule 12 given in Table 5 for Dative case. It is one of generalized rules which are valid in many cases such as derivation of nouns, adjectives and verbs. Some examples are:

bala-Ta→ *bala-Ga*, "to child" (Noun in Dative)
Zaz-TI→ *Zaz-GI*, "of summer" (Adjective)
ZUr-Teli→*ZUr-geli*, "since coming" (Verb)
estit-Tiz→ estit-*kiz*, "make hear"(Causative Verb)

4 Nouns

Nouns in Kazakh Language take singular or plural (A3Sg, A3Pl) suffixes, Possessive suffixes, Case suffixes and Derivational suffixes. In addition, nouns can take Personal Agreement suffixes when they are derived into verbs. For example, *kitap-tar-da-GI-lar-dIN* which means "of those which is in books" has the following morphological analysis

kitap+Noun+A3Pl+Pnon+Loc^DB+Noun+Zero+A3Pl+Pnon+Gen.

Every nominal root at least has form of *Noun+A3Sg+Pnon+Nom.* Therefore, a root noun *kitap* which means "book" has the following morphological analysis

kitap+Noun+A3Sg+Pnon+Nom.

These inflections of noun are given in FST diagram in Figure 1.

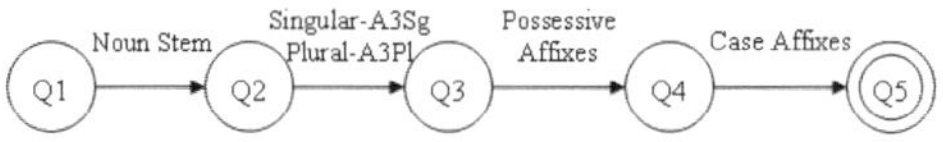

Figure 1. The FSA model of inflectional changes of a noun.

It can be seen that nominal root can be in singular form by adding (+0) no suffix which is in fact third personal singular agreement (A3Sg) and by adding suffix (+PAr) in plural form which is in fact third personal plural agreement (A3Pl). Here *P* is an intermediate level representation letter for *d*, *t* or *l* in surface level. After, possessive affixes (+Pnon:0, +P1Sg:Hm, +P2Sg:HN, +P2PSg:HNJz, +P3Sg:sJ, +P1Pl:HmJz, +P2Pl:HN, +P2PPl:HNJz, +P3Pl:s) and case affixes (Nom, Dat, Abl, Loc, Acc, Gen, Ins) are added. Here *H* and *J* are intermediate letters. All morphotactic rules together with adjective, pronoun, adverb and numerals are given in Figure 2. It can be observed that every adjective can be derived to noun and nouns with relative affix can be derived to adjectives. There are other derivations which are produced by adding some specific suffixes between verbs and nouns, adjectives and adverbs, adjectives and nouns. In order to get rid of complex view those derivations are not explicitly shown in Figure 2.

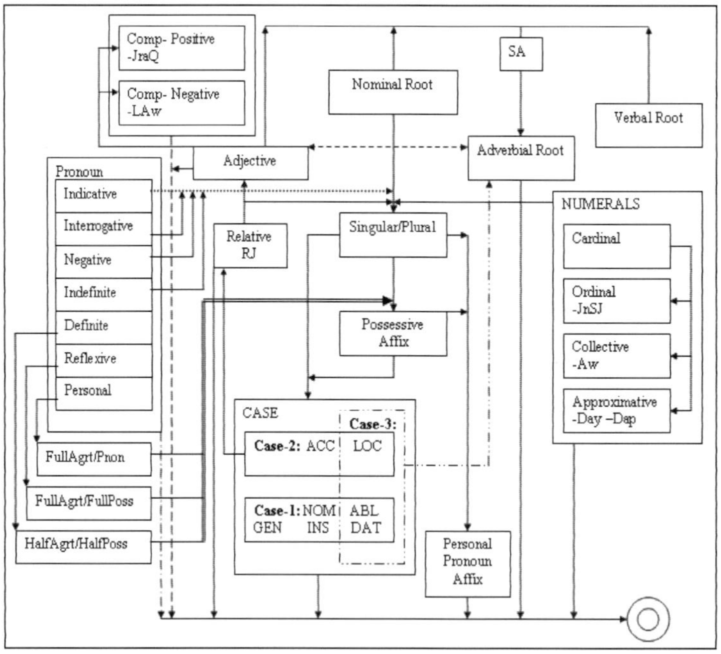

Figure 2. Morphotactic Rules for Nominal Roots.

In our system, the root of a word is a starting point for morphemes defined in lexicon file, and other morphemes are added according to morphotactic rules. Thus, starting from a root the system checks for all possible following morphemes and if a word is matched it gives appropriate output and moves to next state. For example, a surface form of a word *kitaptan*, "from a book" will have intermediate form of "kitap+tan" after implemented alternation rules. First it will check and find a noun root from lexicon. Then after giving output as "*kitap+Noun*", continues with next state which is *Singular/Plural*. At this state it will go on with 0 input giving output of *+A3Sg* for singular form of noun. Then, the next state will be *Possessive Affix* state to determine the personal possessive suffix. Here it is 0, thus epsilon transition which gives output as *+Pnon*. Now the output is *"kitap+Noun+A3Sg+Pnon"*. The next state is *Case* state in order to recognize the case of noun. Thus, for given input such as *+tan*, the output is determined as *+Abl* and this continues until the system reaches the final state or invalid state which is unacceptable state not returned to user. All possible morphemes are defined in the lexicon and all states are visualized in Figure 2.

	Saq/Tense	Suffix
Future	bolZamdI keler Saq *Future Indefinite Tense*	ar/er/r
Future	maqsattI keler Saq *Future Goal Oriented Tense*	baq/bek paq/pek maq/mek
Future / Present	auIspalI keler (osI) Saq *Future (Present) Transitional Tense*	a/e/y
Present	maqsattI osI Saq *Present Goal Oriented Tense*	qalI/galI keli/geli
Present	naq osI Saq *Present Definite Tense*	Ip/ip/p
Present	dEl osI Saq *Present Progressive*	da/de
Past	Zedel Otken Saq *Past Definite Tense*	dI/di tI/ti
Past	auIspalI Otken Saq- Past *Transitional Tense*	atIn/etin ytIn/ytin
Past	ayGaqtI burINGI Otken Saq *Past Narrative Definite Tense*	Gan/gen qan/ken
Past	ayGaqsIz burINGI Otken Saq *Past Narrative Indefinite Tense*	Ip/ip/p

Figure 3. Tenses of Verbs in Kazakh Language.

5 Verbs

Verbs are terms which define actions and states. Mainly three tenses exist such as present, future and past as stated in Figure 3. Moreover, conditional, optative and imperative moods are also defined. However in detailed form there are thirteen tenses together with modals in Kazakh language. These tenses are worked out from many resources where presentation and naming have variance among each other according to their scholars (Tuymebayev, 1996; Mamanov, 2007; Isaeva and Nurkina, 1996; Musaev, 2008). For example, according to Isaeva and Nurkina (1996) *awIspalI keler Saq* "Future Transitional Tense" denotes action in future and has same affix as Present Tense. However, Mamanov (2007) pointing out that *awIspalI keler Saq,* "Future Transitional Tense" denotes present action. Additionally, there are large amount of auxiliary verbs which define tenses and some modal verbs. However in cases that auxiliary verbs are not used verbs become as deverbial adverbs or participles which define verb or noun (Demirci, 2006). In Figure 4, morphotactic rules of verbs and modals are given. Derivations of verbs to nouns and adverbs with specific suffixes are shown with asterisk in Figure 4.

Verbs can be in reflexive, passive, collective and causative forms. For instance, verb *tara-w* means "to comb", *tara-n-w* in reflexive infinity form, *tara-l-w* in passive infinity form, *tara-s-w* in collective infinity and *tara-tQJz-w* and *tara-tTJr-w* in causative infinity form. Here, *Q*, *J* and *T* are intermediate letters. However not all verbs can have all of these forms at the same time.

Verbs in infinity form are generally formed with last letter w. For example: *kelw* which means "to come". The system is performing over generalization on verbs which take auxiliary verb on appropriate tenses. Those verbs are analyzed as derived adverbs or incomplete verbs on that tense since every verb of sentence should have personal agreement at the end and personal agreement affix added to the verb itself after the suffix of tense or to the auxiliary verb. In constructed morphological analyzer, we make analysis of every single word and for that reason generalization of some rules are made by giving more than one result.

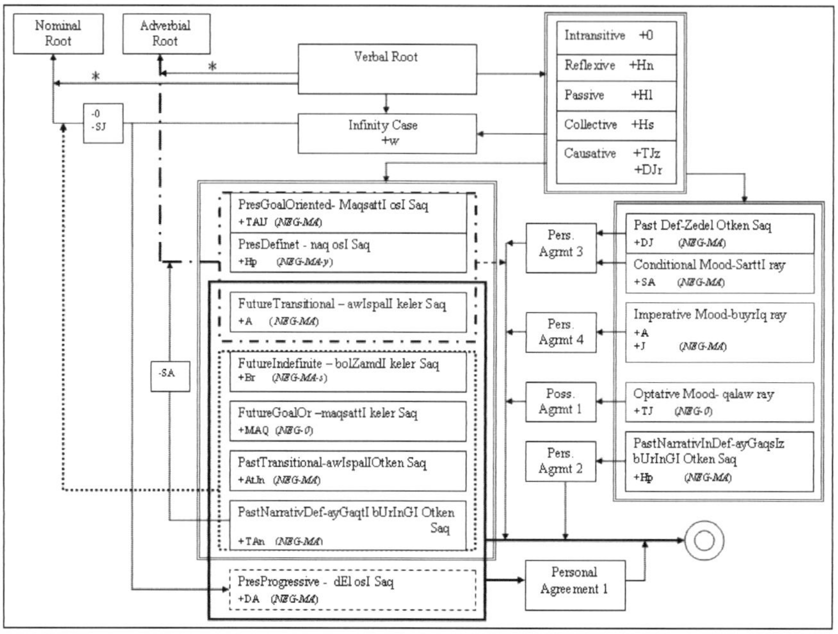

Figure 4. Morphotactic Rules of Verbs in Kazakh Language.

For example, *kel-geli tur-mIn* means "I am planning to come". Here *tur* is an auxiliary form which actually defines the tense of the verb and takes personal agreement affix *mIn*. Without an auxiliary verb, the word *kel-geli* means "since coming" and derived as an adverb. Thus compound verbs are examined separately. Some of tenses have different personal agreement endings and they are presented in Figure 4

6 Tests and Analysis

As mentioned before, the system is implemented using Xerox finite-state tools for NLP. Morphotactic rules and possible morphemes are defined in lexicon file and compiled with lexc tool. Alternation rules are defined in regex file and rule transducer is composed with lexicon file in one network with xfst tool. Loan words, proper names and technical terms are not included. System is working in two directions as in lexical and surface level. Due to the ambiguities in language there is no one-to-one mapping between surface and lexical forms of words and the system can produce more than one result.

A large corpus of Kazakh words (Qazinform, 2010) not seen by the morphological analyzer before has been continually analyzed in order to enhance the system by adding new words to lexicon. There are approximately 1000 words randomly selected from web which exist in lexicon and analyzed with the system. The percentage of correctly analyzed words is approximately 96%. Most of the errors are mainly the errors that occurred in the analysis of technical words which do not obey alternation rules of Kazakh Language. In Table 6, the w1.txt file has more technical words than w2.txt file. The results of the tests are given in Table 6. Errors due to Rules are exception errors which are not included in transducer yet. We hope in near future enhancing of the system will be performed by including all these rules. Also it can be seen in Table 6 that Kazakh words have 2.1 morphologic parses on average.

Files	**Total Words**	**Correctly Analyzed Words**	**Total Errors**	
			Rules	**Analyzer**
w1.txt	1000	962	30	8
w2.txt	1010	978	26	6
Morphologic Ambiguity is 2.1				

Table 6. Test Results.

7 Conclusion

Language is one of the main tools for communication. Thus its investigation provides better perspectives on all other aspects related with NLP. However, formalization and computational analysis of Kazakh language morphology is not widely worked out. In other words, there is a lack of tools for analysis of Kazakh language morphology from computational point of view. Moreover, grammar resources contain variances depending on scholars. For example, in some resources there are twelve tenses, whereas in others there are much less tenses of verbs. Naming of tenses can also vary from source to source. To summarize, building correctly working system of morphological analysis by combining all information is valuable for further researches on language.

In this paper, a detailed morphological analysis of Kazakh language has been performed. Also, a formalization of rules over all morphotactics of Kazakh languages is worked out. By combining all gained information, a morphological analyzer is constructed. For future work, enhancing of system by adding exception rules related with loan words and proper names should be performed. Having more stabilized system with lessened possible rule errors some internal details of character encoding will also be solved. Moreover, releasing the working system to users on the web and collecting feedbacks are intended. These feedbacks from users can help on improving the system capacity and lessen any possible errors. This is planned to be performed with using an open source environment which is alternative to Xerox XFST, namely Foma by Hulden (2009).

Reference

Altenbek G and Wang X. 2010. Kazakh Segmentation System of Inflectional Affixes. *Proceedings of CIPS-SIGHAN Joint Conference on Chinese Language Processing* (CLP2010), Beijing, China, p.183–190.

Altintas K. and Cicekli I. 2001. A Morphological Analyser for Crimean Tatar. *Proceedings of the 10th Turkish Symposium on Artificial Intelligence and Neural Networks (TAINN'2001)*, North Cyprus, p.180-189.

Beesley R. K. and Karttunen L. 2003. *Finite State Morphology*. CSLI Publications, Stanford, CA, USA.

Coltekin C. 2010. A Freely Available Morphological Analyzer for Turkish. *Proceedings of the 7th International Conference on Language Resources and Evaluation (LREC'10)*, Valletta, Malta.

Demirci K. 2006. *Kazakh Verbal Structures and Descriptive Verbs*. Dunwoody Press, Maryland, USA.

Isaeva S, Nurkina G. 1996. *Sopostavitelnaya tipologiya kazakhskogo i russkogo yazykov*. Uchebnogo Posobie. Sanat publishers, Almaty, Kazakhstan.

Hamzaoğlu I. 1993. *Machine translation from Turkish to other Turkic languages and an implementation for the Azeri language.* Master's thesis, Bogazici University, Turkey.

Hulden M. 2009. Foma: a finite-state compiler and library. *Proceedings of the 12th Conference of the European Chapter of the Association for Computational Linguistics: Demonstrations Session.* Association for Computational Linguistics, pp. 29–32.

Kairakbay M. B. and Zaurbekov D. L. 2013. Finite State Approach to the Kazakh Nominal Paradigm. *Proceedings of the 11th International Conference on Finite State Methods and Natural Language Processing (FSMNLP 2013)*, Scotland.

Mamanov I.E. 1961. *Kazahskij jazyk*. Uchebnogo posobie gumanitarnogo tipa. Almaty, Kazakhstan.

Mamanov I.E. 2007. *Qazaq til biliminin maseleleri*. Aris publishers, Almaty, Kazakhstan

Mussayev M. K. 2008. *The Kazakh Language*. Vostochnaya literatura publishers, Moscow, Russia.

Oflazer K. 1994. Two-level Description of Turkish Morphology. *Literary and Linguistic Computing*, 9(2):137-148.

Orhun M., Tantuğ C., Adalı E., and Sönmez C. 2009. Computational comparison of the Uyg-hur and Turkish Grammar. *The 2nd IEEE International Conference on Computer Science and Information Technology*, pp:338-342, Beijing, China.

Qazinform. 2010. National news agency. `http://www.inform.kz/qaz.`

Salimzyanov I, Washington J. and Tyers F, 2013. A free/open-source Kazakh-Tatar machine translation system. *Machine Translation Summit XIV*, Nice, France.

Tantug C., Adali E. and Oflazer K. 2006. Computer Analysis of the Turkmen Language Morphology. *Lecture Notes in Computer Science*, 4139:186-193. A. C.

Tantug C., Adali E. and Oflazer K. 2007. AMT system from Turkmen to Turkish employing finite state and statistical methods. *Proceedings of MT Summit XI.*

Tuymebayev Q. Zhanseyit 1996. *Qazaq Tili: Grammatikaliq anaiqtagish.* Almaty, Kazakhstan.

Valyaeva T., 2014. *Kazakhskii yazyk.* `http://www.kaz-tili.kz/.`

Rules, Analogy, and Social Factors codetermine past-tense formation patterns in English

Péter Rácz
New Zealand Institute of
Language Brain and Behaviour,
University of Canterbury
peter.racz@

Clay Beckner
New Zealand Institute of
Language Brain and Behaviour,
University of Canterbury
clayton.beckner@
canterbury.ac.nz

Jennifer B. Hay
New Zealand Institute of
Language Brain and Behaviour,
University of Canterbury
jen.hay@

Janet B. Pierrehumbert
Department of Linguistics / NICO
Northwestern University.
New Zealand Institute of
Language Brain and Behaviour,
University of Canterbury
jbp@northwestern.edu

Abstract

We investigate past-tense formation preferences for five irregular English verb classes. We gathered data on a large scale using a nonce probe study implemented on Amazon Mechanical Turk. We compare a Minimal Generalization Learner (which infers stochastic rules) with a Generalized Context Model (which evaluates new items via analogy with existing items) as models of participant choices. Overall, the GCM is a better predictor, but the the MGL provides some additional predictive power. Because variation across speakers is greater than variation across items, we also explore individual-level factors as predictors. Females exhibited significantly more categorical choices than males, a finding that can be related to results in sociolinguistics.

1 Introduction

In this report, we present a psycholinguistic study of English past tense categories, using a nonce-probe experiment implemented on Amazon Mechanical Turk. The English past tense has been a testing-ground for a wide range of theories and predictions in psycholinguistics, including the processes of acquisition, the nature of lexical representation, and the representation of inflectional patterns as rules or as generalizations over specific items (Bybee and Slobin, 1982a; Rumelhart and McClelland, 1985; McClelland and Patterson, 2002; Albright and Hayes, 2003).

The present study investigates the factors influencing patterns of preferred past tense forms for particular verb classes. English past tenses are not merely a memorized list, but rather, verb categories can shrink, or expand to include new items. In everyday speech, there is evidence of ongoing influences from multiple verb classes, as verbs exhibit variation and slowly shift in their usage (*dived* vs. *dove*, *sneaked* vs. *snuck*), (Haber, 1976; Bybee and Moder, 1983).

Given that speakers can adapt their verbal categories to new situations, what is the best representation for the relevant morphological generalizations? In analogical models, the focus is on existing stored items in memory. The acceptability of a candidate past tense formation pattern for a particular candidate item is determined by patterns of similarity to stored items. Morphological innovation and productivity arises from generalizations over existing forms in the lexicon. To account for a speech error such as *glew* as the past tense of *glow* (Bybee and Slobin, 1982a), an analogical explanation would highlight the close similarity between *glow* and the present tense forms *blow, throw, know*, which provide the basis for an analogy with the past forms *blew, threw, knew*. Of particular interest is the Generalized Context Model (GCM) (Nosofsky, 1990; Albright and Hayes, 2003), an analogical model which assesses a category's suitability to a target item on the basis of feature-based similarities summed over category items, in addition to the category's size. It has already been successfully applied to model regular and irregular patterns in Arabic morphology (Dawdy-Hesterberg and Pierrehumbert, 2014).

Rule-based approaches propose more abstract representations of generalizations. Originally proposed to handle broadly applicable default patterns, (such as 'add *-ed* to express the past tense'), rule-based approaches have recently been extended to incorporate multiple stochastic rules. Albright and Hayes (2003) assign scores to morphological rules by training a Minimal Generalization Learner (MGL) over a dataset, an algorithm that iterates over pairs of words in the lexicon, hypothesizing generalizations conservatively on the basis of any phonological features that are

Proceedings of the 2014 Joint Meeting of SIGMORPHON and SIGFSM, pages 55–63,
Baltimore, Maryland USA, June 27 2014.

shared across the words. A rule is scored according to how many items it applies to in the lexicon, weighted against cases in which the inferred phonological context is present but the rule fails to apply. The resulting system consists of a catalog of weighted natural class-based generalizations which compete with one another, and which are more or less likely to apply in various phonological contexts (for regular as well as irregular verbs). Albright and Hayes argue that the MGL outperforms the GCM in predicting participant behavior in a nonce-verb production task they conducted.

2 Experiment

We collected a large amount of data on irregular past tense formation in English with a nonce probe test, a classic method for exploring the productivity of inflectional morphology (Berko, 1958). Earlier studies used 30 or fewer participants per condition (Bybee and Slobin, 1982a; Albright and Hayes, 2003). By using Amazon Mechanical Turk, a burgeoning forum for psycholinguistic research (Munro et al., 2010), we were able to recruit a large number of participants and explore the role of individual-level factors in the choice of morphological patterns. Moreover, we tested participant preferences across a large dataset (316 nonce verbs) based on broad phonological sampling within verb classes, allowing for repeated trials across similar items for each participant.

Participants in our online study were presented with a forced choice task in which they had to pick either the regular or the irregular past tense form for an English nonce verb, presented in a carrier sentence. This was followed by a vocabulary task in which participants had to rate the familiarity of English nouns.

2.1 Stimuli

We set up five categories of irregular past tense formation based on phonological form of the present tense verb, and its corresponding candidate tense past forms. Each category exhibits phonological variability within the category, while also allowing for a specific phonological description. We avoided 'miscellaneous' verb classes, as well as wholly idiosyncratic patterns (such as *go–went*). Moreover, we are particularly interested in morphological classes which are known to display some indeterminacy (Haber, 1976), i.e., those classes which display some regular/irregular variation (*dived* vs. *dove*), due to the ready availability of multiple generalizations. The literature contains various taxonomies of English irregular verb classes (Bybee and Slobin, 1982a), but our current classification mostly represents a subset of the detailed verb classes outlined by Moder (1992).

The five categories of interest are as follows.

- **SANG**. Verbs that form the past tense with a vowel change from [ɪ] to [æ] (e.g. *sing–sang, sink–sank, swim–swam*).

- **BURNT**. Verbs that form the past tense by adding a [t], with no change in the stem vowel (e.g. *burn–burnt, spill–spilt, learn–learnt*). These items constitute a distinct set from regular English pasts such as *boss–bossed* which are articulated with a [t] allomorph, insofar as the **burnt** verb bases actually end in a voiced consonant but are nonetheless affixed with a voiceless stop.

- **KEPT**. Verbs that form the past tense by adding a final [t] and changing the stem vowel from [i] to [ɛ] (e.g. *keep–kept, mean–meant, feel–felt*).

- **DROVE**. Verbs that form the past tense with a vowel change from [aɪ] or [i] to [oʊ] (e.g. *drive–drove, weave–wove, ride–rode*).

- **CUT**. No-change past tense verbs, that is, verbs the past tense form of which is identical to their present tense form. (e.g. *cut–cut, cost–cost, hurt–hurt*). Verb bases in this class end in sounds that are already associated with the English past tense ([t] or [d]) (Bybee and Slobin, 1982a), although the nonce verb bases in the present study all end in [t].

We generated nonce verb forms by combining the category-specific restrictions spelled out above on the stem with a set of syllable onsets that occur in English. Using CELEX (Baayen et al., 1993), we then filtered the orthographic and phonetic transcriptions of the nonce stems, as well as the resulting past tense forms, to exclude real English words. Two native speakers checked the final list to remove additional real words that were not filtered out via the CELEX database (e.g., slang and informal terms). All our verb forms were monosyllabic– as are almost all English irregular verbs in general. The method used to generate the stimuli means that some nonce forms looked more similar to real English verbs than others. This way we can tell whether similarities to a single form will strongly influence people's behavior in the case where the nonce form is highly similar to a single real form.

The **sang** and **cut** categories consist of 60 forms. The **burnt** category has 40, **drove** has 76, and **kept** has 80. The total number of nonce verbs is 316.

2.2 Setup

The experiment consisted of a forced choice task, in which participants had to pick a regular or irregular past tense form for each verb. Verbs were presented one at a time, visually, in a carrier sentence of the form 'I really like to VERB. Yesterday, I   .'. Two buttons were presented under the carrier sentence, one with the regular past tense, adding *-ed*, and one with the irregular past tense. The irregular past tense was always the dominant pattern for the category. (So, for **cut**, it was identical to the present tense, etc.) The order of the two buttons was randomized for each verb. Each verb was presented once and the order of verbs was randomized for each participant.

The experiment was appended by a word familiarity rating task. The rating task was based on Frisch and Brea-Spahn (2010). It consisted of 50 nouns of varying familiarity, as well as 10 extremely common nouns and 10 nonce words. The 70 words were presented in a random order. The participant had to select, on a scale of 1-5, how familiar the given word was. Incorrect answers to the extremely common nouns and the nonce words were used as an exclusion criterion. Answers for the other items were used as an index of vocabulary level, which is predicted to affect morphological choices in both the GCM and MGL models.

2.3 Participants

111 people took part in the experiment on Amazon Mechanical Turk during the course of two days. 51 were women, 60 were men, and 1 did not specify. The age range of the participants was 20-65, and the mean age was 34. All participants were native speakers of American English. Participants were paid three dollars. We excluded ten participants from the analysis because they failed to differentiate familiar from unfamiliar words in the vocabulary test.

Category	Experiment	Nonce Examples
drove	0.52	skride: skrode, skrided
sang	0.58	sking: skang, skinged
kept	0.59	skeep: skept, skeeped
burnt	0.67	skurn: skurnt, skurned
cut	0.83	skast: skast, skasted

Table 1: Categories and mean regularization ratings.

2.4 Results

The nonce verb categories have different rates of regular vs. irregular usage, as can be seen in Table 1. The *Experiment* column shows the mean regularization rates of the categories in our experiment. The **drove** class was regularized the least often, and the **cut** class the most often, with a considerable difference between the two.

The trends across verb classes are similar to those of Moder's (1992) nonce experiment. Note in particular the high regularization rate (83%) of the no-change class of verbs (**cut**). A search of CELEX indicates that no-change [t]-final verbs are quite widespread in English, represented by more than 30 types. Yet based on nonce responses, the English no-change pattern is not very prone to being applied to novel items. This finding matches observations by Bybee (1982b) that the no-change verb class has been on the decline in English, as evident from increasing regularization. One noteworthy feature of the **cut**-type verbs is that the phonological shape of the base is a quite unreliable indicator of verb class. That is to say, there are many [t]- final verb stems which typically take the regular -ed suffix (e.g., *gritted, salted, blasted*, and these provide counterexamples to the no-change pattern (cf. Moder (1992) on cue validity).

We fit a simple stepwise logistic mixed-effects regression model to the results with a maximal random effects structure, using regularization of individual verb form (yes or no) as an outcome variable and category as predictor. This model confirms the general finding that there is significant variation across the verb classes. (Significance values reported are based on difference with the **sang** class.) The **cut** class shows the highest rate of regularization ($p<0.001$), followed by the **burnt** class ($p<0.01$). It is followed by the **sang** and **kept** classes (these two do not differ significantly). The **drove** class shows the lowest rate of regularization ($p<0.01$).

Participant gender, age, and vocabulary size are not significant predictors of regularization in the simple logistic mixed effects model. However an examination of the data (Figure 1) reveals that for each verb class, variation across subjects is considerably greater than variation across items. This observation suggests that individual traits may play a role in morphological choices in a way that the simple model fails to capture. We will return to this issue after presenting the GCM and MGL model fits, and will find in the end that gender does affect response patterns.

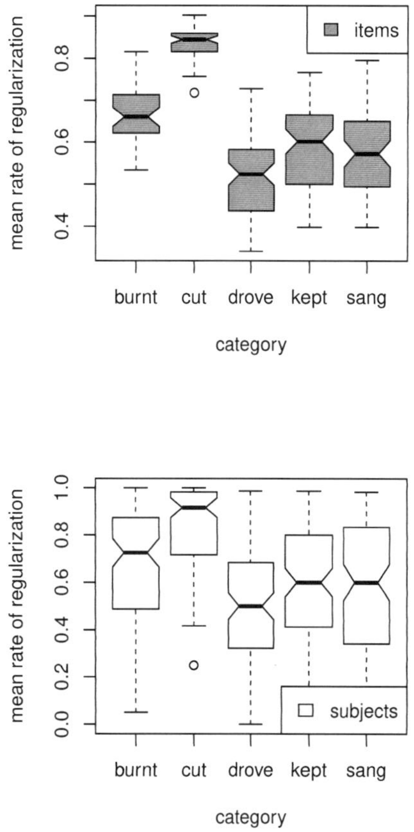

Figure 1: Across-item variation in regularization rates across category (above). Across-subject variation in regularization rates across category (below).

3 Algorithmic Learning Models

We now turn our attention from the baseline effects of category variables, to investigate the predictions of particular algorithmic learning models that provide alternate representations for generalizations on the basis of similarity. Our analyses focus on the predictions of the Minimal Generalization Learner and the Generalized Context Model (Albright and Hayes, 2003; Nosofsky, 1990).

3.1 The two models

The Minimal Generalization Learner (MGL) (Albright and Hayes, 2002; Albright and Hayes, 2003) is an algorithm for inferring stochastic morphophonological generalizations over a set of training items (e.g., paired present and past tense forms). For each pair of items in the lexicon, the learner maximally aligns wordforms and analyzes shared phonetic features, thereby merging word-specific rules (*ring/rang* and *stink/stank*) into rules that express the most general applicable environment: [ɪ] → [æ] / [+coronal, + cont] ___ [ŋ].

Each rule inferred in this way is then further generalized on the basis of more comparisons; for instance, taking note of *swim/swam* expands the [ɪ] → [æ] rule to specify that it occurs before all [+nasal] consonants. The algorithm thus infers a set of natural-class based generalizations, which are weighted by comparing the number of hits for the past tense pattern (*ring/rang, drink/drank, sing/sang, stink/stank, swim/swam*, etc.) divided by the number of cases in which the alternation fails to apply although it *could* apply (thus tallying exceptions such as *think* and *blink*). This appproach favors generalizations that cover many cases, but penalizes those that are too broad because their phonetic environments encompass many exceptions. The MGL reliability metric is further adjusted to a confidence score, in which generalizations that apply to a smaller number of word types are penalized.

Note that the MGL algorithm automatically groups together items on the basis of shared phonological properties; thus, monosyllabic verbs are most likely to form strong generalizations with other monosyllabic verbs. Attempts to merge diverse wordforms under a single generalization would be more likely to incur penalties (i.e., exceptions). This feature of the MGL is important for comparing with the methods of the GCM (see below). Both algorithms allow for category-specific similarities to play a role.

The Minimal Generalization Learner is implemented here from materials made available by Albright and Hayes (2003), including their Segmental Similarity Calculator based on Frisch et al. (2004). The MGL is trained on regular and irregular English verbs with a minimum frequency cutoff of 10 in COBUILD (Baayen et al., 1993), and excluding prefixed verb forms, thus encompassing 4253 past/present verb transcriptions. The MGL is implemented here with its default settings, which includes a lower 75% confidence interval for purposes of adjusting the reliability score.

The Generalized Context Model (GCM) is an instance-based model of categorization. To assign category membership to a novel instance, it first calculates its similarity to instances in preexisting categories. Then, it selects the category with members that are most similar to the novel instance (Nosofsky, 1990). Our implementation of the GCM has three notable aspects to it.

First, we used the GCM to categorize our nonce verb stimuli, basing the categories on real English verb types extracted from CELEX (as with the MGL). Second, we used the same segmental similarity calculator developed and used by Albright and Hayes and used by the Minimal Generalization Learner to calculate the similarity of phonetically transcribed word forms to each other, so that we could take the phonetic similarity of speech sounds into account instead of calculating similarity between word forms based on edit distance alone. We did not weight parts of the word forms differently, because there is evidence that although past tense formation in English is predominantly driven by similarities in word endings, onsets also play a role. (cf. the predominance of s+stop onsets in irregular verbs forming the past tense with a vowel change, e.g. *sing*, *sink*, etc.) (Bybee and Moder, 1983).

Third, our implementation of the GCM reflected the structure of the task. Recall from Section 2 that participants were presented with the stems of the nonce verbs in a sequence and had to pick either a regular or an irregular past tense form for them. The irregular past tense form was predetermined by category, so that, for a given verb, the participants could only choose between the regular past tense form or the irregular past tense form we assigned to the verb. (So, for instance, for *spling*, they could choose either *splinged* or *splang*, but not *splung* or *splingt*, etc.) For a given category (such as *sang* verbs), the GCM had a choice between two sets. The irregular set consisted of verb types in CELEX that form their past tense according to the pattern captured by the category (such as an [ɪ]–[æ] alternation). The regular set consisted of verb types that have a stem that matches the category (such as 'monosyllabic and stem vowel [ɪ]') but have a regular past tense. The model calculated the similarity of a given nonce verb to these two sets (depending on its category). In this paper, we report on category weights assigned to the *regular* category, which are comparable with both the results of the Minimal Generalization Learner and the rate of regularization in our experiment. We only used monosyllabic verbs in identifying relevant matches, for regular as well as irregular items.

Values reported here were generated with no frequency cutoff. Alternate runs with the frequency threshold enforced produce no change in the model. The model is run with the default parameter settings of $s = 0.3$, $p = 1$ with respect to calculating the weighted similarities between items. When p is set to 1, as here, the similarity function is exponential, rather than Gaussian. The weighting parameter s controls the tradeoff in the relative importance of the size of the verb category (the 'gang size') vs. the amount of similarity (measured via edit distance between phonological forms) (Nosofsky, 1990; Nakisa et al., 2001; Albright and Hayes, 2003; Dawdy-Hesterberg and Pierrehumbert, 2014).

Figure 2 shows three plots. The first one depicts the relationship between the predictions of the GCM (regular category weight) and experimental ratings (mean participant regularization) for individual verb types used in the experiment. The Spearman rank correlation is highly significant ($\rho = 0.497$, $p < 0.001$). The second one depicts the relationship between the MGL model predictions (reliability rating of the regular form) and mean participant regularization in the experiment. The Spearman rank correlation between these variables is highly significant ($\rho = 0.393$, $p < 0.001$). The predictions of the two models are z-scored to allow for comparability. The third plot shows the relationship between the predictions of the GCM and the MGL for individual verb types in the experiment. The Spearman rank correlation between these variables is highly significant

CATEGORY	GCM	MGL
SANG	**0.65**	0.55
CUT	**0.18**	-0.19
DROVE	0.37	**0.64**
KEPT	**0.52**	0.18
BURNT	**0.48**	0.24
ALL	***0.5***	0.39

Table 2: Correlations table: Spearman's rank correlations between mean regularization in the experiment and the predictions of the two models

(rho = 0.347, $p < 0.001$), but the correlation is far from perfect. Comparing the overall correlations and patterns in Figure 2, it appears that the GCM is doing a better job of predicting the variation across items than the MGL is. We now turn to an examination of the predictions within our verb classes.

3.2 Model comparisons within verb class

Table 2 shows Spearman rank correlations between mean regularization in the experiment and the predictions of the two models for the five verb categories. Overall, GCM does a better job. The no-change (*cut*) verb class is especially illustrative of the differences between the two models. Note that the MGL is negatively correlated with our experimental data for this category. As noted above, this verb class appears to be strikingly non-productive; participants display a strong preference for regularizing a wide range of t-final forms. The MGL underestimates the regularization of nonce verbs that resemble *cut* and *hit*, while overestimating the regularization of forms like *vurt, slurt, plurt*. The no-change irregular form of such verbs must be modeled on a pattern with a sole English exemplar (*hurt–hurt*), and the Minimal Generalization model (in contrast with the GCM) is swayed very little in such cases. This is one of several cases where the GCM predicts subject preferences better than the MGL does, seemingly because the irregular form requires modeling a response on a sole exemplar.

There is one verb category where the MGL outperforms the GCM: the **drove** class. Here, the MGL does especially well because it makes an accurate prediction about one subcategory of items: nonce verbs like *quine* and *sline* are regularized by participants (*quined,slined*) more often than other members of the **drove** class. Here, it seems that

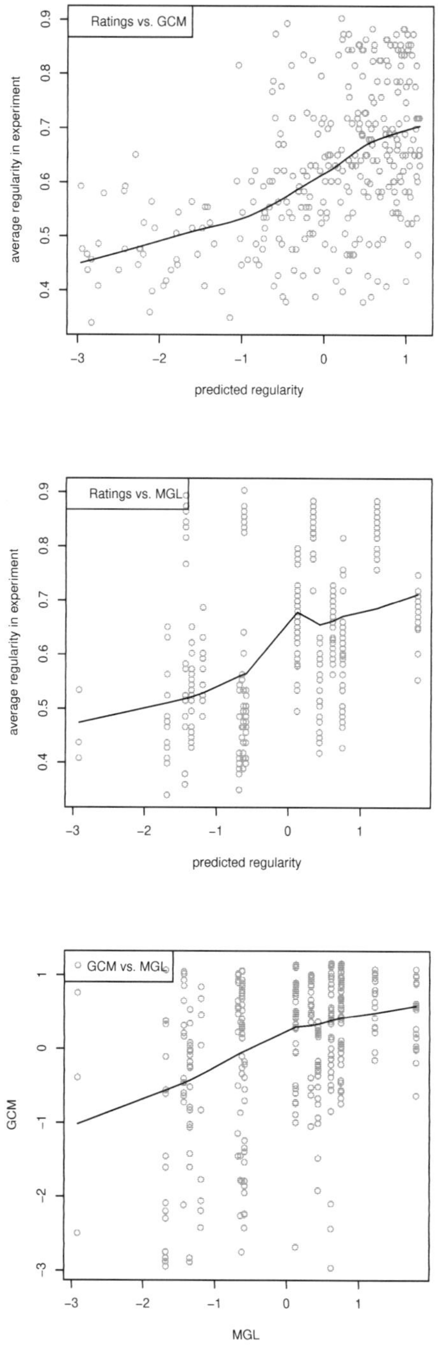

Figure 2: Above: experimental ratings versus GCM predictions. Middle: experimental ratings versus MGL predictions. Below: MGL predictions vs. GCM predictions. (With lowess lines added.)

the irregular past would need to be modeled on one closely-related English item (*shine–shone*), but similar English verbs offer many exceptions to any abstract generalization (*line–lined, mine–mined, whine–whined*, not to mention the transitive verb *shine–shined*). Such a situation causes the MGL to correctly classify all *-ine* final verbs as highly prone to regularization, because *-ine/-one* type irregulars are all dispreferred in the experiment. However, the GCM makes a wide range of predictions for these stimuli on the basis of different segmental similarities with training items (e.g., based on the syllable onsets).

On the whole, comparing the two models on the verb classes suggests that analogy to individual instances is a better approximation of the behavior of our subjects than recourse to abstract generalizations. It is true, however, that both the GCM and the MGL each only explain a part of the observed variance. In order to test whether the two models contribute differently to explaining participant behavior in our dataset, we fitted a simple stepwise logistic mixed-effects regression model on the results with maximal random effects structure, using regularization on the individual verb form (yes or no) as an outcome variable. Instead of verb category, we used the GCM and the MGL regularization rates as predictors. Both predictors are significant. An analysis of variance test reveals that the regression model that includes the predictions of both categorization models provides a significantly better fit than the models including either alone. We tested nonlinear effects of MGL and GCM, using restricted cubic splines, but nonlinearity did not significantly improve the model. Participant age and gender are not significant. Vocabulary size explains some variation, though does not quite meet the threshold of .05 for significance. The interaction of GCM predictions and participant gender, however, is significant. The model coefficients can be seen in Table 3.

Predictor	b	z	sig.
(Intercept)	0.71	4.5	***
MGL	12.4	3.38	***
GCM	1.11	5.05	***
gender (male)	-0.02	-0.07	(n.s.)
vocabulary	-0.25	-1.77	.
GCM : gender (male)	0.47	2.12	*

Table 3: Effects of rules vs. analogy in the regression model

3.3 Individual-level factors

As both MGL and GCM make reference to existing patterns in the lexicon, we hypothesized that the precise size and contents of an individual's vocabulary is likely to produce individual variation in terms of the lexical support available for certain patterns. Individuals with higher vocabulary scores may be more likely to have robust stored instances of irregular, lower frequency, minority past tense patterns. We might therefore predict that they are more accepting of irregular realizations. This is, to some degree, confirmed by the strength of vocabulary as a predictor of regularization in our final model. A potential interaction of vocabulary size and the two models of past tense formation is that these models likely have different predictions when trained on vocabulary sets of various sizes – this is a clear direction of future research.

We also tested the effects of participant gender, as women have been reported to be more biased towards more standard language (Labov, 2001). This would mean that conformity to speech community standards in whether a form is irregular or regular (essentially, getting it 'right') could be highly valued by women. Consistent with this observation, we find a significant interaction between GCM and participant gender. Females show a steeper slope for the GCM than the males do. When there is low analogical support for regularization, females have a tendency to prefer irregular forms more than males do, but this difference is reversed for items where the GCM provides strong support for the regular. In that case, females prefer regular forms more than males do. To put it differently, females categorize the verb forms more in our dataset than the males do.

It is interesting to note that our results differ from Hartshorne and Ullman's (2006) child data on real English verbs. They found more over-regularization for girls than for boys. The mechanism they suggest relies on girls having more precocious verbal ability, as is commonly reported. These results may seem hard to reconcile, since the adult women in our study did not regularize more than men (there was no significant overall effect of gender), nor did they have larger vocabularies, as measured by our vocabulary inventory. However, they are compatible if we assume that the real verbal lexicon is rather well learned by adulthood (as reflected in the weakness of vocabulary level as a statistical predictor in our model) and that the gender difference we observed taps the social factors mentioned by Labov, which are learned gradually during childhood and adolescence.

4 Conclusions

Our results suggest that both the GCM and MGL models contribute important insights into factors underpinning perceived wellformedness. Individuals are heavily influenced by the combined analogical force of existing lexical forms. They generalize over items. However, they also, it appears, generalize over these generalizations - forming more abstract 'rules' or associations that operate in parallel with the token-based analogical processes. While this seems to be the interpretation that is pointed to by this current data set, verification of the joint role of these types of processes clearly requires a lot more explicit testing in different and varied data sets, including real verbs in addition to nonce forms. Recent models in phonological processing and speech perception certainly point to a hybrid model, in which instance-based processing and reasoning sits alongside more abstract structures, and in which both types of processes may be jointly operative – with the balance affected by many factors including the particular nature of the task at hand (Pierrehumbert, 2006). Indeed, we would predict that it should be possible to design morphological tasks which more readily tap into purely analogical processes, or into more abstract generalizations.

Acknowledgments

This project was made possible through a grant from the John Templeton Foundation. The opinions expressed in this publication are those of the authors and do not necessarily reflect the views of the John Templeton Foundation. Hay and Beckner were also supported by a Rutherford Discovery Fellowship awarded to Hay. The authors would like to thank Adam Albright, Patrick LaShell, Chun Liang Chan, and Lisa Garnard Dawdy-Hesterberg. All faults remain ours.

References

Adam Albright and Bruce Hayes. 2002. Modeling English past tense intuitions with minimal generalization. In *Proceedings of the ACL-02 workshop on Morphological and phonological learning-Volume 6*, pages 58–69. Association for Computational Linguistics.

Adam Albright and Bruce Hayes. 2003. Rules vs. analogy in English past tenses: A computational/experimental study. *Cognition*, 90(2):119–161.

R Harald Baayen, Richard Piepenbrock, and Rijn van H. 1993. The CELEX lexical data base on CD-ROM.

Jean Berko. 1958. The child's learning of English morphology. *Word*, 14:150–177.

Joan L Bybee and Carol Lynn Moder. 1983. Morphological classes as natural categories. *Language*, pages 251–270.

Joan L Bybee and Dan I Slobin. 1982a. Rules and schemas in the development and use of the English past tense. *Language*, pages 265–289.

Joan L Bybee and Dan I Slobin. 1982b. Why small children cannot change language on their own: Suggestions from the English past tense. In *Papers from the 5th international conference on historical linguistics*, volume 21.

Lisa Garnand Dawdy-Hesterberg and Janet B Pierrehumbert. 2014. Learnability and generalisation of Arabic broken plural nouns. *Language, Cognition and Neuroscience*, (ahead-of-print):1–15.

Stefan A Frisch and Maria R Brea-Spahn. 2010. Metalinguistic judgments of phonotactics by monolinguals and bilinguals. *Laboratory Phonology*, 1(2):345–360.

Stefan Frisch, Michael Broe, and Janet Pierrehumbert. 2004. Similarity avoidance and the OCP. *Natural Language and Linguistic Theory*, 22:179–228.

Lyn R Haber. 1976. Leaped and leapt: a theoretical account of linguistic variation. *Foundations of Language*, pages 211–238.

Joshua K Hartshorne and Michael T Ullman. 2006. Why girls say holded more than boys. *Developmental Science*, 9(1):21–32.

William Labov. 2001. *Principles of linguistic change Volume 2: Social factors*. Blackwell.

James L McClelland and Karalyn Patterson. 2002. Rules or connections in past-tense inflections: What does the evidence rule out? *Trends in cognitive sciences*, 6(11):465–472.

Carol Lynn Moder. 1992. *Productivity and categorization in morphological classes*. Ph.D. thesis, State University of New York at Buffalo.

Robert Munro, Steven Bethard, Victor Kuperman, Vicky Tzuyin Lai, Robin Melnick, Christopher Potts, Tyler Schnoebelen, and Harry Tily. 2010. Crowdsourcing and language studies: the new generation of linguistic data. In *Proceedings of the NAACL HLT 2010 Workshop on Creating Speech and Language Data with Amazon's Mechanical Turk*, pages 122–130. Association for Computational Linguistics.

Ramin C. Nakisa, Kim Plunkett, and Ulrike Hahn. 2001. A cross-linguistic comparison of single and dual-route models of inflectional morphology. *Peter Broeder, & Jaap Murre, Models of Language Acquisition: Inductive and Deductive Approaches*, pages 201–222.

Robert M Nosofsky. 1990. Relations between exemplar-similarity and likelihood models of classification. *Journal of Mathematical Psychology*, 34(4):393–418.

Janet B Pierrehumbert. 2006. The next toolkit. *Journal of Phonetics*, 34(4):516–530.

David E Rumelhart and James L McClelland. 1985. *On learning the past tenses of English verbs*. Institute for Cognitive Science, University of California, San Diego.

10 Open Questions in Computational Morphonology

Grzegorz Kondrak
Department of Computing Science
University of Alberta
gkondrak@ualberta.ca

Abstract

The objective of this paper is to initiate discussion within the SIGMORPHON community around several issues that involve computational morphology, phonology, phonetics, orthography, syllabification, transliteration, machine translation, inflection generation, and native language identification.

1 Morphology in Machine Translation

In contrast with English, which is a morphologically simple language, many languages have dozens of different wordforms for any given lemma, some of which are unattested even in large monolingual corpora. In Statistical Machine Translation (SMT), lexical sparsity in such languages is often addressed by performing morphological segmentation, which simplifies the correspondence between the tokens in the source and target language. When translating into English from a morphologically complex language, the segmentation is a form of preprocessing performed before the the translation process. Since the English words are not segmented, the output of the decoder can be directly compared to the reference translation. However, when translating in the opposite direction, the segmentation must be reversed to make the generated text readable. *Desegmentation* is typically performed as a post-processing step that is independent from the decoding process. Unfortunately, the pipeline approach may prevent the desegmenter from recovering from errors made by the decoder, including output morpheme sequences that cannot be combined into valid words.

Salameh et al. (2014) propose to replace the pipeline approach with a solution inspired by finite-state methods. They perform desegmentation directly on the search graph of a phrase-based decoder, which is represented as a *lattice* encoding a large set of possible decoder outputs. The lattice, which can be interpreted as a finite–state acceptor over target strings, is composed with a *desegmenting transducer* which consumes morphemes and outputs desegmented words. The desegmenting transducer, in turn, is constructed from a table that maps morpheme sequences to words. The lattice desegmentation algorithm effectively combines both segmented and desegmented views of the target language, and allows for inclusion of features related to the desegmentation process, as well as an unsegmented language model. The results on English-to-Arabic indicate significant improvements in translation quality. However, the morphology of Arabic is largely concatenative, with relatively simple morpheme-boundary adaptations. In contrast, many European languages are classified as *inflecting*, with affixes that represent several rather than a single morpheme. The question remains whether a morphologically-aware approach can be developed to improve translation into inflecting languages as well.

2 Inflection Generation

An alternative to the morphological segmentation approach is to reduce the diverse forms in the training bitext to lemmas, and, at test time, reconstruct the wordforms in the target language directly from lemmas annotated with morphological features. Note that the wordforms that have not been seen in training pose a problem for language models, and are typically shunned by the current SMT systems.

Although complex morphology leads to a high type-to-token ratio, words tend fo fall into certain inflectional paradigms. Individual inflections are obtained by combining a specific affix with a stem. These combinations are rarely concatenative, often affecting characters at the end or even in the middle of a stem.

Proceedings of the 2014 Joint Meeting of SIGMORPHON and SIGFSM, pages 64–68,
Baltimore, Maryland USA, June 27 2014.

For languages without hand-built morphological analyzers and generators, automated learning of morphological paradigms is the only option. Dreyer and Eisner (2011) propose a Dirichlet process mixture model and loopy belief propagation to learn complete paradigms starting from an initial small set of seed paradigms. An unannotated corpus is utilized to guide the predictions of the model by reducing the likelihood of generating unseen wordforms. Durrett and DeNero (2013) align the lemmas with inflected forms to identify spans that change for the inflections, and learn explicit rules for applying those changes in contexts in which they appear. Their joint model is aware of complete paradigms, and is able to correct errors made on individual inflections.

Nicolai et al. (2014) train a discriminative string transducer on lemma-inflection pairs, and apply a separate re-ranking step to take advantage of the paradigmatic constraints. In spite of its relative simplicity, their string transduction approach outperforms the previous approaches to learning morphological paradigms on several European languages. The question remains whether the string transduction approach is also superior to more complex methods on languages with different morphological systems.

3 From Syntax to Morphology

In some languages, syntactic function of phrases is mainly marked by word position and prepositions, while other languages rely on morphology to a greater degree. Similarly, verbal attributes such as tense, person, and gender, can be either encoded morphologically or lexically. Chahuneau et al. (2013) propose a discriminative model for translating into morphologically rich languages that predicts inflections of target words from source-side annotations that include POS tags, dependency parses, and semantic clusters. In other words, they exploit the syntax of the source language to select the most likely wordforms in the target language,

The open question in this case is whether instead of learning a prediction model separately for each language pair, the morphological features could be mapped directly on the source words. For example, in the phrase *she would have asked*, the actual morphological marking is minimal, but the context disambiguates the person, number, gender, and aspect of the verb. Explicit morphological annotation could not only help machine translation, but also provide a rich source of information in the monolingual context, which would go well beyond POS tagging.

4 Transliteration and Morphology

Transliteration is sometimes defined as "phonetic translation" (Knight and Graehl, 1997). In fact, it is straightforward to train a transliteration model using SMT toolkits by treating individual characters as words, and words as sentences. However, unless substantial modifications are made, the accuracy of such a system will be mediocre. Transliteration needs a dedicated approach in order to fully exploit the source-side context and other constraints.

The way we define tasks in NLP is important, because the definitions (and shared tasks) tend to guide research in a particular direction. New papers are expected to show improvement over previously published results, preferably on already established benchmarks. Redefining a task carries the risk of being interpreted as an attempt to avoid a fair experimental comparison, or as a misdirected effort to investigate irrelevant problems.

The NEWS Shared Task on Machine Transliteration was held four times between 2009 and 2012 (Zhang et al., 2012). With the exception of the 2010 edition that included a transliteration mining task, the shared task was invariably defined in terms of learning transliteration models from the training sets of word pairs. This framework seems to ignore the fact that many of the transliteration target words can be found in monolingual corpora, in a marked contrast with the prevalent SMT practice of avoiding unseen words. Cherry and Suzuki (2009) show that the inclusion of a target lexicon dramatically improves transliteration accuracy. Unfortunately, the paper has largely been ignored by the transliteration community (perhaps because it strays from the standard task formulation), as well as the SMT community (perhaps because it shows only modest gains in terms of BLEU score).

Another drawback of limiting the training data to a list of name pairs is the lack of the context that is required to account for morphological alterations. For example, the title of the Russian Wikipedia page that corresponds to *Presidency of Barack Obama* back-transliterates as *Presidentstvo Baraka Obamy*, where the personal name appears in the genetive case. Simply including morphological variants in the training data without their context is likely to confuse a transliteration model. How to best combine transliteration with morphology remains an open question.

5 Transliteration and Orthography

Transliteration is more than just phonetic translation. In the idealized model of Knight and Graehl (1997) a human transliterator pronounces a name in the source language, modifies the pronunciation to fit the target language phonology, and writes it down using the orthographic rules of the target script. In reality, however, the source orthography strongly influences the form of the transliteration. For example, the Russian transliteration of the name *Dickens* on Wikipedia back-transliterates as *Dikkens*, although *Dykynz* would be much closer to the original pronunciation. For less well-known names that first appear in English-language news, human transliterators are often in the dark because the correct pronunciation may be difficult to guess from the spelling.

Al-Onaizan and Knight (2002) report that a spelling-based model outperforms a phonetic-based model even when pronunciations are extracted from a pronunciation dictionary. Bhargava and Kondrak (2012) present a re-ranking approach that is able to improve spelling-based models by consulting the supplied pronunciations. It remains an open question how to design a superior joint model that would generate transliterations directly from both spelling and pronunciation.

6 Transliteration and Decipherment

Although transliteration is typically defined as conversion between writing scripts, the proper form strongly depends on the particular target language with its phonological and orthographic constraints. For example, the name of the city that hosted the recent Winter Olympics is represented in various European languages as *Sochi*, *Sotchi*, *Sotschi*, *Sotsji*, *Sotji*, *Sotši*, *Soči*, *Soczi*, *Szocsi*, etc. In order to derive language-specific transliteration models, we would need to collect training data for thousands of possible language pairs.

Ravi and Knight (2009) introduce the task of unsupervised transliteration without parallel resources. They formulate the problem as decipherment, and reconstruct cross-lingual phoneme mapping tables from Japanese words of English origin, achieving approximately 50% character accuracy on U.S. names written in the Katakana script.

Hauer et al. (2014) frame transliteration as a substitution cipher, and apply a mixture of character- and word-level language models to the decipherment of a known language written in an unknown script. The authors treat a short text in Serbian as enciphered Croatian, and attempt to recover the "key", which is the mapping between the characters in the two writing scripts. In reality, Croatian and Serbian are distinct but closely related languages, that are written in different scripts and exhibit differences in both lexicon and grammar. In particular, 30 Serbian Cyrillic characters correspond to 27 letters in Croatian Latin, with three of the characters represented in the other script as digraphs (e.g., *nj*). The decipherment error rate plateaus at about 3% at the ciphertext length of 50 words. In contrast, a pure frequency-based approach fails on this task with a mapping error rate close to 90%. The question remains whether a more flexible approach could be applied successfully to unsupervised transliteration of languages that are less closely related.

7 Phonetic Similarity of Translations

Words that are phonetically similar across different languages tend to be transliterations, or at least share the same origin. For this reason, words on two sides of a bitext are more likely to correspond to each other if they exhibit phonetic similarity (Kondrak, 2005). This is true even for completely unrelated languages because of the prevalence of loanwords, proper names, and technical terms. Orthographic similarity, which reflects phonetic similarity, has been exploited in the past to improve word and sentence alignment in SMT, and other NLP tasks.

Surprisingly, the correlation with phonetic similarity appears to hold for any translations, defined as words that express the same meaning in some context. Kondrak (2013) observes that even after all cognates and loanwords are removed from consideration, the similarity between the words from different languages for the same concept is significantly higher on average than the similarity between the words for different concepts (as measured by the Longest Common Subsequence Ratio). This seems to contradict the Saussurean principle of the arbitrariness of the linguistic sign.

Kondrak (2013) proposes to explain this phenomenon by positing a chain of correlations between the following word characteristics: translatability, frequency, length, and similarity. The key observation is that translations are on average closer in terms of their length than random words. First, pairs of cross-lingual translations exhibit a correlation with respect to the logarithm of their frequencies. Intuitively, translations refer to the same semantic concepts, which tend to be expressed with similar frequency across languages. Second, the connection between word frequency and length is well established (Zipf, 1936). Finally, pairs of words that differ in length are less likely to be considered similar, which is reflected by word similarity measures. In summary, the reason for the greater phonetic similarity of translations lies in the similarity of their frequencies, which is reflected by the similarity of their lengths. This hypothesis remains to be verified on other languages and data sets.

8 L1 Phonology in L2

The task of Native Language Identification (NLI) is to determine the first language (L1) of the writer of a text in another language (L2) (Tetreault et al., 2013). Koppel et al. (2005) report 80% accuracy in classifying a set of English texts into five L1 languages using a multi-class linear SVM with features including function words, POS bigrams, and character n-grams. Tsur and Rappoport (2007) observe that limiting the set of features to the relative frequency of the 200 most frequent character bigrams yields a respectable accuracy of about 65%. They interpret this as evidence that the choice of words in L2 is strongly influenced by the phonology of L1. As the orthography of alphabetic languages is representative of their phonology, character bigrams appear to capture these phonetic preferences.

In order to test the above hypothesis, Nicolai and Kondrak (2014) design an algorithm to identify the most discriminative words and the corresponding character bigrams. They find that the removal of such words results in a substantial drop in the accuracy of the classifier that is based exclusively on character bigrams, and that the majority of the most indicative character bigrams are common among different language sets. They conclude that the effectiveness of a bigram-based classifier in identifying the native language of a writer is primarily driven by the relative frequency of words rather than by the influence of the phonology of L1. Although this provides evidence against the hypothesis of Tsur and Rappoport (2007), the question to what degree the L1 phonology affects L2 writing remains open.

9 English Orthography

The English spelling system is notorious for its irregularity. Kominek and Black (2006) estimate that it is about 3 times more complex than German, and 40 times more complex than Spanish. This is confirmed by lower accuracy of letter-to-phoneme systems on English (Bisani and Ney, 2008). A survey of English spelling (Carney, 1994) devotes 120 pages to describe phoneme-to-letter correspondences, and lists 226 letter-to-phoneme rules, almost all of which admit exceptions.

In view of this, the claim of Chomsky and Halle (1968) that English orthography is "close to optimal" could be interpreted as facetious. The question is how we could validate the accuracy of this statement from the computational perspective. It would seem to require answering at least the following three questions: (a) what is the optimal orthography for English, (b) how to measure the distance between alternative orthographies, and (c) what distance should be considered "close".

10 Syllabification and Morphology

Orthographic syllabification of words is sometimes referred to as hyphenation. Bartlett et al. (2008) propose a sequence prediction approach to syllabify out-of-dictionary words based on letter n-gram features. Despite its high accuracy, their system suffers from the lack of awareness of compound nouns and other morphological phenomena. For example, *hold-o-ver* is incorrectly syllabified as *hol-dov-er*.

Yao and Kondrak (2014) demonstrate that the accuracy of orthographic syllabification can be improved by using morphological information. In particular, incorporating oracle morphological segmentation substantially reduces the syllabification error rate on English and German. If unsupervised segmentation is used instead, the error reduction is smaller but still significant. However, they are unable to achieve any error reduction using a *supervised* segmentation approach, even though it is much more accurate than the unsupervised approach. The confirmation and explanation of this surprising result remains an open question.

References

Yaser Al-Onaizan and Kevin Knight. 2002. Machine transliteration of names in Arabic texts. In *Workshop on Computational Approaches to Semitic Languages*.

Susan Bartlett, Grzegorz Kondrak, and Colin Cherry. 2008. Automatic syllabification with structured SVMs for letter-to-phoneme conversion. In *ACL*, pages 568–576.

Aditya Bhargava and Grzegorz Kondrak. 2012. Leveraging supplemental representations for sequential transduction. In *NAACL-HLT*, pages 396–406.

Maximilian Bisani and Hermann Ney. 2008. Joint-sequence models for grapheme-to-phoneme conversion. *Speech Communication*, 50(5):434–451.

Edward Carney. 1994. *A Survey of English Spelling*. Routledge.

Victor Chahuneau, Eva Schlinger, Noah A. Smith, and Chris Dyer. 2013. Translating into morphologically rich languages with synthetic phrases. In *EMNLP*, pages 1677–1687.

Colin Cherry and Hisami Suzuki. 2009. Discriminative substring decoding for transliteration. In *EMNLP*, pages 1066–1075.

Noam Chomsky and Morris Halle. 1968. *The Sound Pattern of English*. Harper & Row.

Markus Dreyer and Jason Eisner. 2011. Discovering morphological paradigms from plain text using a Dirichlet process mixture model. In *EMNLP*, pages 616–627.

Greg Durrett and John DeNero. 2013. Supervised learning of complete morphological paradigms. In *NAACL-HLT*, pages 1185–1195.

Bradley Hauer, Ryan Hayward, and Grzegorz Kondrak. 2014. Solving substitution ciphers with combined language models. Submitted for publication.

Kevin Knight and Jonathan Graehl. 1997. Machine transliteration. In *ACL*, pages 128–135.

John Kominek and Alan W. Black. 2006. Learning pronunciation dictionaries: Language complexity and word selection strategies. In *HLT-NAACL*, pages 232–239.

Grzegorz Kondrak. 2005. Cognates and word alignment in bitexts. In *MT Summit*, pages 305–312.

Grzegorz Kondrak. 2013. Word similarity, cognation, and translational equivalence. In Lars Borin and Anju Saxena, editors, *Approaches to Measuring Linguistic Differences*, pages 375–386. De Gruyter Mouton.

Moshe Koppel, Jonathan Schler, and Kfir Zigdon. 2005. Determining an author's native language by mining a text for errors. In *SIGKDD*, pages 624–628.

Garrett Nicolai and Grzegorz Kondrak. 2014. Does the phonology of L1 show up in L2 texts? In *ACL*.

Garret Nicolai et al. 2014. In preparation.

Sujith Ravi and Kevin Knight. 2009. Learning phoneme mappings for transliteration without parallel data. In *NAACL*, pages 37–45.

Mohammad Salameh, Colin Cherry, and Grzegorz Kondrak. 2014. Lattice desegmentation for statistical machine translation. In *ACL*.

Joel Tetreault, Daniel Blanchard, and Aoife Cahill. 2013. A Report on the First Native Language Identification Shared Task. In *Workshop on Innovative Use of NLP for Building Educational Applications (BEA8)*.

Oren Tsur and Ari Rappoport. 2007. Using classifier features for studying the effect of native language on the choice of written second language words. In *Workshop on Cognitive Aspects of Computational Language Acquisition*, pages 9–16.

Lei Yao and Grzegorz Kondrak. 2014. In preparation.

Min Zhang, Haizhou Li, A Kumaran, and Ming Liu. 2012. Report of NEWS 2012 machine transliteration shared task. In *4th Named Entity Workshop*, pages 10–20.

George Zipf. 1936. *The Psychobiology of Language*. Routledge.

Author Index